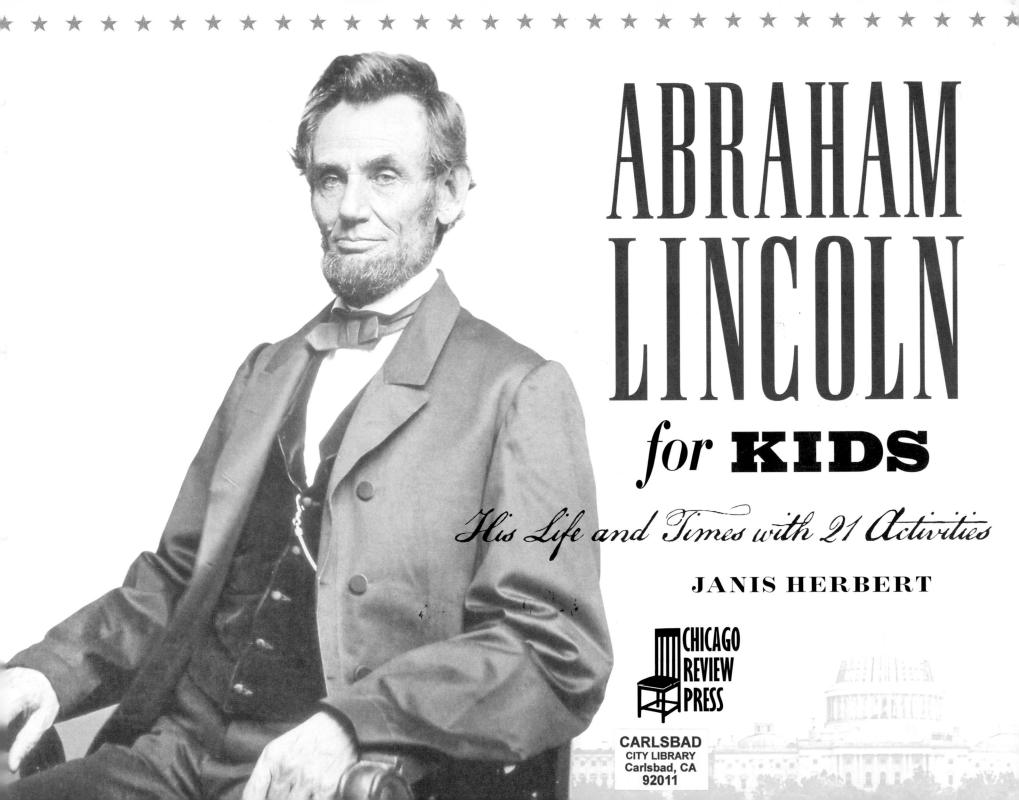

ABRAHAM LINCOLN

for KIDS

His Life and Times with 21 Activities

JANIS HERBERT

CHICAGO REVIEW PRESS

Library of Congress Cataloging-in-Publication Data

Herbert, Janis, 1956-
  Abraham Lincoln for kids : his life and times with 21 activities / Janis Herbert.— 1st ed.
     p. cm.
  Includes bibliographical references and index.
  Audience: 9 and up.
  ISBN-13: 978-1-55652-656-5
  ISBN-10: 1-55652-656-3
  1. Lincoln, Abraham, 1809-1865—Juvenile literature. 2. Presidents—United States—Biography—Juvenile literature.
3. Creative activities and seat work—Juvenile literature. I. Title.

E457.905.H47 2007
973.7092—dc22
[B]

2007009052

COVER AND INTERIOR DESIGN: Monica Baziuk
INTERIOR ILLUSTRATIONS: Laura D'Argo
COVER PHOTO CREDITS: Abraham Lincoln (center) courtesy of the Library of Congress. Model of a log cabin
(bottom right) courtesy of Jeff Herbert. (On the left-hand side down from the top.) The first reading of the
Emancipation Proclamation courtesy of the Library of Congress. Freedom quilt courtesy of Jeff Herbert. Mary
Todd Lincoln courtesy of Library of Congress. Ulysses S. Grant and his Generals on horseback courtesy of
the Library of Congress. Chief Black Hawk courtesy of the Library of Congress. Knob Creek, Kentucky, cabin
courtesy of Jeff Herbert. Lincoln and Hamlin flag courtesy of the Library of Congress.

NOTE TO THE READERS: To see the sources of the quotes in this book,
visit www.janisherbertforkids.com.

© 2007 by Janis Herbert
All rights reserved
First edition
Published by Chicago Review Press, Incorporated
814 North Franklin Street
Chicago, Illinois 60610
ISBN-13: 978-1-55652-656-5
ISBN-10: 1-55652-656-3
Printed in China

5   4   3   2   1

For Jeff, "my all."

CONTENTS

ACKNOWLEDGMENTS

WITH GRATITUDE TO Tom Daggett, Sara Dickinson, Kent Fevurly, Karen Freschauf, Sue Kuehl, Debbie Lenny, Cheryl Mendel, Martha Nowak, Anne Rumery, Stanley Wernz, and Vicki Shaw-Woodard for inspiration, enthusiasm, research, and resources, all graciously given. Special thanks to Tim Ross, whose photographs appear in this book, for his great talent and his companionship on trips to Springfield. Thanks to Ian Herbert for the tour of Washington, to Patti Sorokin for the joke, and to Jeanine Musial for the laughs. I am grateful that this book was in the expert hands of designer Monica Baziuk, and grateful, too, to work with the dedicated, kind, and professional people of Chicago Review Press, especially Devon Freeny, Jon Hahn, and Cynthia Sherry. With each of my books, I become more grateful for supportive parents Ruth and Don Ross, who never miss an opportunity to help. Every writer should have a spouse like Jeff Herbert, who tracked down books and articles, read numerous drafts, corrected my mistakes, and tried out the crafts. For all of that, for his support and patience and love, and for building more than one beautiful log cabin, I am immeasurably grateful.

INTRODUCTION

"**E**VERYBODY IN THE world knows Pa used to split rails!" said Abraham Lincoln's son Tad. But in 1861, as Lincoln made his way to the White House, people knew little else about the president-elect. He didn't like to talk much about his childhood. He had been a rail splitter, a storekeeper, a one-term congressman, and a lawyer. He was the husband of Mary Todd and the father of four boys, one deceased. Newspapers even got his name wrong.

Many despaired at the surprising election of this obscure Illinois man. One newspaper called him an ignorant backwoods lawyer. Few suspected that he could succeed in holding the United States together. The nation, struggling over the issues of slavery and states' rights, was fragmenting.

Across the nation, churches and communities split. Family members argued; deep ties were broken. In Washington, congressmen and senators argued and even came to blows over the country's differences. The best political minds had failed. Decades of effort and compromise had come to nothing.

As Lincoln's train moved east to Washington, Southern states broke their ties to the Union and declared themselves a new nation, the Confederate States of America. As Lincoln entered the White House, Confederate guns pointed toward a federal fort in South Carolina.

The country was in an uproar. All turned their eyes to the tall, ungainly Lincoln and wondered how he could lead them out of this crisis. Who was this Abraham Lincoln?

"The dogmas of the quiet past are inadequate to the stormy present. The occasion is piled high with difficulty, and we must rise to the occasion. As our case is new, we must think anew, and act anew."

—Abraham Lincoln

TIME LINE

1809 FEBRUARY 12 Abraham Lincoln is born

1816 DECEMBER Lincoln family moves to Indiana

1818 OCTOBER Nancy Hanks Lincoln (Abraham's mother) dies

1819 DECEMBER Thomas Lincoln (Abraham's father) marries Sarah Bush Johnston

1828 JANUARY Sarah Lincoln (Abraham's sister) dies

APRIL Lincoln journeys by flatboat to New Orleans

1830 MARCH Lincoln family moves to Illinois

1831 MARCH Lincoln's second flatboat journey to New Orleans

JULY Lincoln moves to New Salem, Illinois

1832 MARCH Lincoln runs for state legislature

1832 APRIL–SEPTEMBER Lincoln fights in Black Hawk War

1834 AUGUST Lincoln is elected to Illinois House of Representatives (serves four terms)

1837 MARCH Lincoln becomes an attorney

APRIL Lincoln moves to Springfield

1842 NOVEMBER Lincoln and Mary Todd marry

1843 AUGUST Robert Todd Lincoln is born

1846 MARCH Edward Baker "Eddy" Lincoln is born

AUGUST Lincoln is elected to the U.S. House of Representatives

1850 FEBRUARY Eddy Lincoln dies

DECEMBER William Wallace "Willie" Lincoln is born

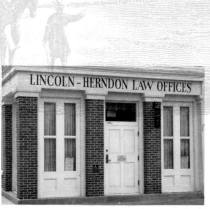

LINCOLN - HERNDON LAW OFFICES

1851 JANUARY Thomas Lincoln dies

1853 APRIL Thomas "Tad" Lincoln is born

1855 FEBRUARY Lincoln loses race for Senate

1858 AUGUST–OCTOBER Lincoln-Douglas debates

1860
NOVEMBER Lincoln loses Senate race to Douglas
MAY Lincoln is nominated for presidency
NOVEMBER Lincoln is elected president

1861
FEBRUARY Lincoln leaves Springfield
MARCH 4 Lincoln is inaugurated in Washington
APRIL 12 Civil War begins

1862 FEBRUARY Willie Lincoln dies

1863
JANUARY 1 Lincoln signs Emancipation Proclamation
NOVEMBER 19 Lincoln gives Gettysburg Address
DECEMBER 8 Lincoln issues proclamation of amnesty and reconstruction

1864
JULY 11–12 Lincoln comes under fire at Fort Stevens
NOVEMBER 8 Lincoln is reelected to presidency

1865
MARCH 4 Lincoln's second inauguration
APRIL 4 Lincoln enters Richmond
APRIL 9 Robert E. Lee surrenders at Appomattox
APRIL 14 Lincoln is shot by John Wilkes Booth
APRIL 15 Abraham Lincoln dies
APRIL 26 John Wilkes Booth killed by federal troops
MAY 4 Lincoln is buried in Springfield, Illinois
DECEMBER 6 13th Amendment is ratified

"ABRAHAM LINCOLN IS MY NAME."

The nickname "Abe" would stick with him all of his life, but Abraham suited the boy better. It was long, like he was. Though still a child, he was already as tall as a man. A-b-r-a-h-a-m L-i-n-c-o-l-n, he would write, with a stick in the dirt, with charcoal on a shovel, with his fingers in the snow. He wrote "anywhere and everywhere," he later said, "that lines could be drawn." Abraham was his grandfather's name, the grandfather who had been killed by Indians. Abraham was a name from the Bible, one of the few books his family owned.

Abraham Lincoln was eight years old before he learned how to write his name. The boy's father could barely sign his own name; his mother, it is thought, could read but not write. For most people on the frontier, schooling was a luxury. There was too much work to be done.

Back in Kentucky, where he was born, Abraham and his big sister Sarah walked two miles to reach their "ABC school." In Indiana, they attended school only now and then. There, Abraham and the other students learned just the most basic reading, writing, and arithmetic. They recited their lessons out loud all day long. "Blab school," they called it, because of the constant noise. Their teacher also tried to teach them manners by having them introduce each other. One student would go outside the log schoolhouse, then come back in the room as if he or she were a great gentleman or lady. Another student escorted the important person around the room, making polite introductions to the others in the class.

Though Abraham loved learning, his parents couldn't always afford to pay the dollar or two it cost per term. Also, they needed him at home to help his father chop wood, fetch water, clear fields of trees and rocks, sow seeds, and help with the harvest. All together, Abraham's formal schooling added up to only about one year.

Abraham and his family had said good-bye to Kentucky when he was seven. The family had been there for two generations, since his grandfather Abraham had learned of the rich frontier land from pioneer Daniel Boone. The elder Abraham and his wife and children settled in the Kentucky wilderness in the late 1700s. Young Abraham Lincoln heard the story many times, of how his grandfather broke land and created a home in the wild western forests. One day, while this earlier Abraham and his three young boys were planting corn, Indians

"Abraham Lincoln Larnin' Ettyket"
❖ Indiana Historical Society

attacked. Abraham was killed. His youngest child, Thomas, leaned over his father's body, heartbroken. The middle child raced to the fort for help while the oldest, Mordecai, managed to hide in a nearby cabin. As Mordecai watched, horrified, an Indian crept up behind his brother Thomas, ready to attack. Mordecai aimed his rifle at the Indian and killed him before Thomas was harmed.

Fatherless, Thomas worked hard to earn a living as a manual laborer and carpenter. Eventually he scraped together enough money to buy his own farm. His neighbors called Thomas "honest" and "plain" and laughed at his good-natured jokes. Thomas married Nancy Hanks, a thin, dark-haired, intelligent woman with sad eyes, and together they made their home in a one-room log cabin near Hodgenville, Kentucky. They named their land Sinking Spring Farm, for the cool spring that provided their water. Their cabin was dark and small with a dirt floor, barely large enough for the family of four—parents, daughter Sarah, and new baby Abraham.

When Abraham was not yet two, the family settled near crystal-clear Knob Creek and built another small log cabin. Steep, tree-covered hills surrounded their home. Neighbors were few, but peddlers, soldiers, and, at times,

Knob Creek, Kentucky ❧ Jeff Herbert

TO MAKE HIS FAMILY'S HOME, Thomas Lincoln stacked notched logs, added a roof, and cut a door. He "chinked" the cabin (filled in cracks and holes) with split pieces of wood and wet clay and grass. Practice with a miniature log cabin—someday you might build a real one of your own!

Adult supervision required

WHAT YOU NEED

- ▨ Rectangular folding cardboard box, 9½ by 12 inches
- ▨ Ruler
- ▨ Pencil
- ▨ Scissors
- ▨ Poster board, 8 by 12 inches
- ▨ Clear packing tape
- ▨ Craft sticks
- ▨ White glue
- ▨ Pliers
- ▨ Emery board
- ▨ Rough brown cloth, 3½ by 4 inches
- ▨ Waxed paper

On one narrow side of the box, measure the top edge of the flap and mark a point at the exact center. Draw lines from that point toward the fold (see drawing). Cut along the lines to make the flap into a triangle. Repeat on the opposite side.

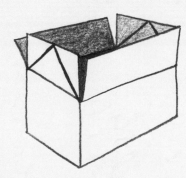

With the triangles standing up, fold the long flaps inward. You will almost have a roof, but there will be a couple of inches of space between the flaps. To fill this gap, set a folded piece of poster board over the top and tape it to the flaps. Cut a 3-by-3½-inch door one craft-stick-length from an end of the box. If you would like a window, cut a 2-by-2-inch square on another side, one craft-stick-length from an end. You might need to ask an adult to help cut through the box.

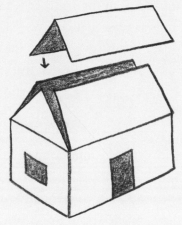

Glue craft sticks horizontally onto the box. To make the cabin look more authentic, stack them so that every other one sticks out slightly over the sides. You might need to cut some of the craft sticks to fill in spaces—have an adult use the pliers to snap off the pieces you need. Sand the edges smooth with an emery board. Continue stacking logs to make a roof.

Glue the cloth to the top of the door (and pretend it's a buffalo-hide covering). Cover the window with waxed paper.

chained slaves passed on the dusty trail near their cabin. Here a baby brother was born, then died. Thomas planted corn and little Abraham followed him, placing pumpkin seeds in the earth.

Though the land was rich, Thomas saw greater opportunity north of the Ohio River. There, in Indiana, land was open for settlement and slavery was against the law. In Kentucky, Thomas had problems getting a clear deed to his farm; another man was claiming his land. And Thomas hated slavery, which was prac-ticed in Kentucky. Hundreds of thousands of black people—some taken by force from their African homelands, others born into slavery—labored on farms and plantations across the southern United States. Considered property, they could be beaten, mistreated, or bought and sold at their owner's will. Thomas wanted no part of this evil institution.

Thomas went to Indiana and laid his claim, then returned to bring his family to their new home site near Pigeon Creek. It was a difficult and long journey on foot and on horseback,

"Picking Cotton on a Georgia Plantation"
❖ Library of Congress

ENSLAVED!

Slavery in America was nearly 200 years old by the time Abraham Lincoln was born. Ever since a Dutch ship brought 20 black slaves to the colony of Virginia in 1619, untold numbers of Africans had been torn from their homes and transported across the ocean to a life of enslavement in a strange land. There, they toiled as farmhands, carpenters, blacksmiths, and personal servants. Many led short, brutal lives of backbreaking labor. They could be branded, whipped, or mistreated, sold at auction and separated from their children, parents, or spouses. Even those who were treated kindly by their masters always knew that their lives would never be their own and that their children, too, would be born and live as slaves.

Before the American Revolution, slavery was legal throughout the colonies. After the Revolutionary War, some of the new states abolished slavery, but the practice continued in the South. When delegates gathered to write the United States Constitution, they argued bitterly about slavery. Many hated it and wanted it completely abolished in their newly created country. But delegates from Southern states said they would never agree to a constitution that interfered with

the practice. Without it, they claimed, their whole way of life would be destroyed. The Southern economy depended on a large labor force to raise crops like cotton, rice, and tobacco.

As a compromise, the delegates agreed that Congress would not interfere with the slave trade for 20 years. Around the same time, Congress passed the Northwest Ordinance. This law stated that when the territories north of the Ohio River and east of the Mississippi River became states, those states would be free.

But slavery continued and even increased, expanding into territories south and west. Cotton became an even more profitable crop after inventor Eli Whitney created the cotton gin, a machine that separated cotton fibers from seeds. With his invention, cotton plantations grew larger and the demand for slaves increased.

Just a year before Abraham Lincoln's birth, the United States government outlawed slave ships from bringing new slaves from Africa. But by that time there were already more than a million slaves in America, and that number grew with illegal shipments of Africans and with every child born to a slave.

then by ferry across the Ohio River. Beyond the river, the country was so heavily wooded and dense with bushes that Thomas had to slash his way through to break a trail for his wife and children. Their new home was a "half-faced camp"—a three-sided shelter made of branches and brush. By then, it was winter. They cut logs and built a cabin, but bitterly cold winds found their way through the chinks in the cabin's walls.

The family lived off the deer and bears their father hunted. Abraham tried to hunt too, but when he succeeded in killing a turkey he was so distressed by the animal's death that he never again "pulled a trigger on any larger game."

Though Indiana had just become a state, this land was still a wilderness, where bears and cougars roamed and wolves howled at night. There were no near neighbors; settlements were few and miles between. The Lincolns and other settlers could only rely on themselves. They made their own log cabins and built rough tables and benches to furnish them. They killed game and gathered wild berries, mushrooms, and nuts, which they ate from wooden or pewter platters. They cleared land, sowed crops, milked cows and raised hogs. They tanned leather to make their own shoes, though it was common to go barefoot in warm weather or even wear shoes made of tree bark. They wore shirts and dresses of home-

spun "linsey-woolsey" (linen and wool woven together). Abraham wore a coonskin cap and deerskin pants, which were always too short for the growing boy, exposing inches of his pale shins.

The Lincoln cabin had a floor of packed earth. There were no windows or even a proper door; inside it was dark and gloomy. Frontier women took their chores outdoors, mending clothes or shucking corn under the shade of a tree. Candles were expensive to make, so indoor light came from the fireplace or a saucer of grease with a floating wick. Most people were so tired after a long day of work that they went to sleep at sunset.

The Lincolns labored to make a farm of the wilderness. Abraham, though only eight years old, was big for his age. His father put an ax in his hands and, as Abraham later described, "from that time until his twenty-third year, he

Nancy Lincoln's grave ❖ Jeff Herbert

was almost constantly handling that most useful instrument." He and his father cleared trees for their farm and planted potatoes, wheat, corn, and squash. After harvest, it was time to grind the wheat and corn. Abraham loaded the family's horse and, alone, led it through the woods to the gristmill. One day at the mill, the horse kicked young Abraham in the head. Hearing the news, Abraham's father ran to the mill and carried the boy home. Abraham lay unconscious all night—"apparently killed," as he later said. But the boy came to life again in the morning, sputtering and yelling to the horse to "git up!"

After a spring and summer of hard work, the family was cheered when Abraham's great-aunt and great-uncle and his cousin Dennis Hanks moved into a nearby cabin. But their good spirits did not last long. Aunt and uncle died from what was called "milk sickness," an illness caused by drinking tainted milk from cows that had eaten a poisonous plant. Soon after, Abraham's gentle and loving mother fell ill. When she knew her death was near, she called her children to her and reminded them to "be good and kind to their father, to one another, and to the world." Her death was a bitter loss for the young boy and his father and sister.

Cousin Dennis moved in with them, and Sarah, only 12, tried to cook and keep house like her mother. When she despaired and sat by the fire crying, her brother and cousin tried to comfort her by bringing her a baby turtle or raccoon. Abraham mourned his "angel mother" and tried to be as good and kind as she would have wanted him to be.

Over a year later, Sarah Bush Johnston came into Abraham Lincoln's life. A widow with three children, she agreed to marry Thomas Lincoln. The Lincoln children and cousin Dennis had lived alone in their cabin while Thomas went to Kentucky to court Sarah, and now he brought her back to Indiana as his new bride. Dennis later remembered how the new Mrs. Lincoln soaped and scrubbed the lonely children clean, and gave them the love and affection they had so much missed. She had her new husband make a proper door and a wooden floor for the cabin, and cut a window hole, which she covered with greased paper (a substitute for glass, which was a rare item in those days). She had him build an attic room, too, where Abraham, his cousin, and his new stepbrother, John, would sleep, climbing up each night on pegs driven into the wall. Her presence made it a happier family. She loved Abe, calling him "the best boy I ever saw or ever expect to see." Abraham called her "Mama" and loved her like his own mother.

Abraham's cousin described everyday life as a constant round of work, as the boys "grubbed, plowed, mowed, and worked together barefooted in the field." But life was brighter now. With his stepmother's encouragement, Abraham attended school. He rushed home to tend to animals and chores. But, cousin Dennis said, "whenever Abe had a chance in the field, while at work, or at the house, he would stop and read." He read while plowing, stopping at the end of each row to rest the horse and snatch a few lines from a book. At home, with a book in his hands and his feet up as high as his head, he ignored everyone around him. Books were scarce but his stepmother had brought several with her from Kentucky. These he pored over again and again. He read the family Bible along with *The Pilgrim's Progress* and *Aesop's Fables*. One of his favorite books was *The Life of George Washington*. "The accounts of

*"Abraham Lincoln is my name
And with my pen I wrote the same
I wrote in both hast[e] and speed
And left it here for fools to read."*

—a rhyme young Abraham Lincoln wrote in his sum book

battlefields and struggles for the liberty of the country" thrilled him, he later said. "There must have been something more than common that those men struggled for."

"When he came across a passage that struck him, he would write it down on boards," said his stepmother. Paper was hard to come by. When the board was black with writing, he whittled it down and used it again. He practiced until he was so good at spelling and writing that neighbors who couldn't write asked him to compose their letters for them.

There were times when Abraham felt troubled. When he was older, he revisited his home in Indiana and recalled his childhood as a time of both pleasure and great sadness. He had lost his mother and had difficulty getting along with his father, who seemed to prefer Abraham's stepbrother, John. Cruelty especially bothered him. Once, when he caught some children building a small fire on top of a tortoise's shell, he made them stop and reminded them that even "an ant's life was to it as sweet as ours to us."

All of his life he would struggle with an underlying sadness, but there was also an unquenchable spark of fun and wit in Abraham Lincoln. For a spellbound audience of family and neighbor children, he would mount a tree stump and mimic long-winded politicians. He told jokes and drawn-out stories, like one about a preacher with a lizard down his shirt. Friendly and kind, he liked to make people feel at ease. When a schoolmate, called on in class to spell, was about to make a mistake, Abraham caught her attention and pointed to his eye to show her that *i* was the letter she needed.

New settlers moved to the Indiana community and Abraham's father hired him out to work for these neighbors. "My how he could chop," one of his neighbors said. "If you heard him felling trees in a clearing, you would say there were three men at work." A day laborer could earn 25 cents a day for chopping trees, removing stumps, digging wells, or building fences. Abraham's hard-earned money went back to support his family. At 16, he was six feet, two inches tall and 160 pounds, with coarse, unruly black hair. His long legs and arms were muscled from hard work. He was wiry and very strong but not eager for a lifetime of backbreaking labor. "My father taught me to work," he joked with a neighbor, "but he never taught me to love it!"

There was no end of work on the frontier. The neighbors helped one another raise cabins, kill hogs, and harvest crops. They made special occasions of their chores, holding corn-shucking parties and quilting bees. Frolics, suppers, wrestling matches, and races followed hard work. Abraham joined in the work, then attracted laughing crowds with his comical stories.

In addition to doing work as day laborer, Abraham helped out at a local blacksmith's shop. He worked for a ferryman on a nearby river. He also built his own boat. In the small river communities of those days, there were no wharves where steamships could dock; boats stopped mid-river and people rowed out to meet them. One day, Abraham rowed two men out to the middle of the Ohio River, where he helped them hoist their trunks aboard a steamboat. When they each tossed him a half-dollar in payment, he couldn't believe his luck. "A dollar in less than a day," he thought. "The world seemed wider and fairer."

But the world turned dark for him at age 18, when his beloved sister, Sarah, died in childbirth. She had married and left home only a year before and he had missed her already. Now she was gone forever. Only months later, Abraham left home himself for the first time.

In those days, the Mississippi River was part of a vital trade route for the western lands of Indiana and Illinois. Grain and meat sent downstream to New Orleans on square, flat-bottomed rafts called flatboats could be sold or traded for luxury goods such as sugar and coffee. Abraham hired on as a Mississippi River flatboatman. Though some flatboats were as much as 100 feet long, complete with a

Traveling on a flatboat ❖ Photograph by Tim Ross

cabin onboard for the crew, his was modest. It carried only him and another young man, and their barrels of meat, flour, and corn. They steered it 1,200 miles down the Ohio River and the wide Mississippi, with its dangerous currents and shifting sandbars.

As the young men made their way downstream, they stopped at river towns to trade along the way. Each night, they tied their boat along the riverbank. One night, they tied up alongside a Louisiana plantation and went to sleep. Seven slaves boarded their flatboat and attacked them, "with intent to rob and kill," Abraham later reported. He and his friend

WITH ONLY TWO OARS and a long "sweep" (for steering), flatboatmen guided their crafts down the Mississippi River. It wasn't possible to row back upstream against the mighty current. Once in New Orleans, flatboatmen broke up their boats and sold the lumber. They hiked home along the long, dangerous road known as the Natchez Trace, or purchased a steamboat ticket back north. Make this miniature flatboat and imagine their adventures!

Adult supervision required

WHAT YOU NEED
- ▨ 1 piece of balsa wood, 3¾ by 4 by 36 inches
- ▨ Ruler
- ▨ Pencil
- ▨ Box cutter or X-ACTO knife
- ▨ White glue
- ▨ Newspaper
- ▨ Toothpicks
- ▨ Small wooden spool

Have an adult cut the balsa wood into the following pieces:

- ▨ for the hull bottom, a 10-by-4-inch rectangle
- ▨ for the hull sides, two 10-by-1-inch pieces
- ▨ for the hull ends, two 4-by-1-inch pieces
- ▨ for the cabin top, a 7-by-2½-inch rectangle
- ▨ for the cabin sides, two 7-by-2-inch pieces
- ▨ for the cabin ends, two 2½-by-2-inch pieces (cut a 1-inch-square door in one of the cabin end pieces)
- ▨ for the oar locks, three pieces ½ by ¼ inch (make a notch in one of the short ends of each)
- ▨ for the oars and sweep, three thin 6-inch sticks and three 1-by-½-inch rectangles

After spreading newspaper over your workspace, glue the hull sides and ends onto the hull bottom. Glue the cabin sides and ends together. Let these pieces dry for a few hours. Glue the roof onto the cabin and let dry.

Glue the cabin inside the hull, spacing it so the end with the door is 2 inches from one end of the hull. Glue two of the oar locks 1½ inches from the front of the cabin, as shown. Glue the other lock in the center of the back of the cabin's roof, as shown. Let dry.

Glue the small rectangles onto the thin sticks to make oars and a sweep. Use toothpicks or leftover scraps of wood to make a ladder. Place it against the cabin and place the oars and sweep in their locks. Glue the small wooden spool in a corner near the door of the cabin. Your pretend flatboatmen can row or steer from the roof or sit on the spool and enjoy the ride!

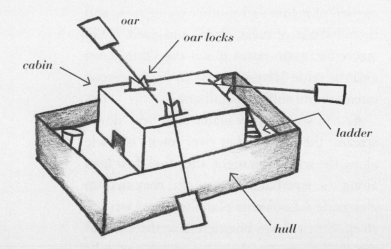

oar
oar locks
cabin
ladder
hull

drove the looters from their boat, cut their cable, and floated downstream to safety.

Back in Indiana, Abraham gave his father the $25 he had earned and returned to work. He began to wonder when he would get his own start in the world. He frequently walked 15 miles to the county seat to watch the local judge hear trials. He spent long hours at the store in the nearby village of Gentryville. Here, he and his friends read newspapers from far-away eastern towns. They argued about politics, and swapped jokes and stories.

In early spring 1830, when Abraham was 21, the Lincoln family sold their land, packed their belongings onto wagons, and left for a new home. Abraham's cousin John Hanks had moved to Illinois, and he sent letters urging the family to follow him. Illinois had rivers and wide, fertile prairie land waiting for settlement. Its abundant forests meant there was plenty of wood for homes, fences, and heating. Settlers poured in to buy up inexpensive land.

Though their spirits were high at the prospects ahead, the Lincoln family met many challenges on their journey. The frozen ground was just starting to thaw under the weak spring sun. Melting snow flooded the rivers and covered the roads. It made slow and muddy going for the oxen and their heavy load. There were no bridges; family and oxen walked across frozen streams or waded through icy cold water.

While crossing one frozen river, Abraham looked back to see that his pet dog had fallen through the ice and was fighting for his life. "I couldn't bear to lose my dog," he later told a friend. He jumped off the wagon, waded waist-high into the icy waters, and pulled his pet to safety.

The family's destination was the Sangamon River, 10 miles from the village of Decatur. It was rough, unsettled country. Most settlers in Illinois lived in the southern part of the state; Chicago was just a camp of a few huts and stores. Decatur consisted of only a dozen log cabins. That summer and fall, the Lincoln family cleared trees and built a cabin. Abraham and his cousin broke the land with oxen and plow, raised a crop of corn, and built a split-rail fence around the 10 acres of their new farm.

That autumn, the whole family suffered from malaria (called ague) and fever. That winter, snowdrifts buried fences, roads, trees, and cabins. The Deep Snow of 1830 began shortly before Christmas and didn't stop for weeks. After three or four feet of snow fell, icy rain covered the drifts. Temperatures dropped to below zero and stayed there for over two months. People huddled in their cabins, cattle froze to death, and wild animals died of starvation. When spring finally came, the melting snow flooded the rivers and countryside.

IN THE HEADLINES

While hanging around the Gentryville store, Abraham and his friends most likely talked about local concerns, like the reappearance of the dreaded milk sickness or neighbors who had pulled up stakes for Illinois. Possibly it was here that they planned elaborate pranks, such as the time Abraham arranged to have two bridegrooms fixed up with the wrong brides on their wedding day. They read newspapers from "back east," and learned about—and talked about—events in the bigger world. What was in the news in those days?

1824: House of Representatives Chooses John Quincy Adams for President ∽ In an exciting presidential race, war hero Andrew Jackson received the most popular votes but did not win in the Electoral College (when electors from each state cast their votes). The fate of the election was turned over to the House of Representatives. They chose John Quincy Adams, son of former president John Adams. Adams's foes called this "the Stolen Election."

1825: Erie Canal Opens ∽ Laborers built channels, locks, aqueducts, and bridges to create a 363-mile waterway between New York's Hudson River and the Great Lakes. In an era before railroads, the Erie Canal opened the western frontier, making it easy and cheap to bring goods across the country.

1826: Thomas Jefferson and John Adams Die on Same Day ∽ In a shocking twist of fate, Founding Fathers and former presidents Jefferson and Adams died within hours of each other—on the 50th anniversary of the signing of the Declaration of Independence.

1828: President Signs "Tariff of Abominations"—Southerners Outraged ∽ Northern manufacturers were happy about the new tariff (import tax) on goods from other countries. It meant more Americans would buy from them instead. In the South, where there wasn't much industry, people hated the tariff. They worried that foreign countries might try to get even with the United States by taxing the South's biggest product—cotton. Angry Southerners threatened to break away from the United States and create their own country.

1828: Andrew Jackson Elected President ∽ Andrew Jackson was famous for defeating the British at the Battle of New Orleans during the War of 1812, and famous too for brawling and dueling. He made a life for himself as lawyer, slave owner, congressman, and judge, then president of the United States. Nicknamed "Old Hickory" because he was as tough as hickory wood, Jackson was a strong and controversial president, much admired and much hated.

1830: Indians to Be Removed to Western Lands ∽ As more white settlers moved onto traditional Indian lands, native peoples were displaced and conflicts increased. The Indian Removal Act gave President Jackson the power to offer land west of the Mississippi River to Indians who left their tribal homelands in the east. Some nations signed and left, if only to keep peace. Others wished to stay but were eventually forced west, walking there on what they called a "Trail of Tears."

With no game to hunt, and a late spring planting season, people went hungry. An outbreak of cholera followed, killing thousands.

Neighbors helped each other through these and other hardships. When winter storms struck, settlers rescued freezing neighbors and revived them at their hearths. They fought through the snow to herd animals to the safety and warmth of their stables. When summer fires whipped across the prairies, people joined forces to stifle the flames with wet sacks. Men gathered for daylong wolf hunts and, with no local government or sheriff, tracked and captured lawbreakers on their own. Women helped each other when malaria struck and acted as midwives for pregnant neighbors. Hardship drove some back to homes east and south. The hardiest stayed and made new lives in Illinois.

The Lincolns stayed. Abraham worked with his father and took on odd jobs for neighbors, but he was restless to get out on his own. When a local trader, Denton Offutt, asked him to take a flatboat of goods down the Mississippi River, he jumped at the chance to get away.

"WORTHY OF THEIR ESTEEM"

Abraham, his stepbrother, and his cousin loaded their handmade boat with pork and corn, then steered down the Sangamon River toward the Mississippi. Near the village of New Salem, Illinois, they tried to run their boat over a dam but failed and got stuck. The front end of the boat hung over the dam. To their alarm, the back began to fill with water! Abraham struggled to wrestle the boat off the dam while a crowd gathered to watch. When muscles didn't work, he used his mind: he moved some of their goods to the front of the boat to lift the back up, drilled a hole in the front to let the water drain out, then plugged the hole back up and eased the boat over the dam. Trader

Denton Offutt was so impressed that he promised the young man another job on their return.

The young men set off for New Orleans, hailing other adventurers on flatboats, keelboats, and timber rafts. Giant steamboats paddled up- and downstream. The Mississippi River flowed through a newly minted America, one full of hope and promise for some but not for all. Settlers found opportunity in the new territories and states. Ambitious men created mills, towns, colleges, and courthouses. But Indians had been pushed off their lands to regions west of the mighty river. And along its banks, planters oversaw the work of slaves, who labored to cut forests and drain swamps.

On this trip downriver, Abraham saw "negroes in chains, whipped and scourged." The state of Missouri, just across the river from Illinois, had been admitted to the Union as a slave state only 10 years before. When the Missouri Territory petitioned for statehood, members of Congress argued furiously over whether it would be a slave or a free state. Northerners insisted that the Northwest Ordinance prohibited slavery north of the Ohio River. Southerners argued that Missouri was actually west of where the Mississippi River ended, so the Northwest Ordinance didn't count. Congressmen debated and argued and fought. It looked as if they would never reach an agreement. Finally, Speaker of the House Henry Clay came

Gristmill in New Salem, Illinois ❖ Jeff Herbert

LINCOLN'S BOAT FLOAT

Remembering how hard it was to pilot a boat in shallow waters, Lincoln later invented a device to help get boats over sandbars. He whittled a model of his invention and patented it (a patent is an assurance from the U.S. government that no one else can make or sell your invention for a period of time). On Lincoln's model, bellows attached to the boat's hull were pumped with air to help raise the boat over sandbars. His model is on display at the Smithsonian's Museum of American History in Washington, D.C.

up with the Missouri Compromise: Missouri would be accepted into the Union as a slave state while the new state of Maine would be free. That way, there would be a balance between slave and free states. Also, the Missouri Compromise stated, from that time on slavery would be outlawed anywhere in the territory north of the 36°30′ latitude line.

In Mississippi, slaves hoed, weeded, and picked cotton, and loaded bales onto passing riverboats. At the crowded Natchez slave market, black women, dressed in calico, and black men, brushed and cleaned to bring a high price, waited silently for their turn on the auction block. On Louisiana sugar plantations, slaves planted, cut, crushed, and boiled cane in the sweltering heat. They worked from sunup to sundown for their masters, then tried to find a few precious hours at dusk to tend their own vegetable patches or hunt for their family's dinner. Late at night, they gathered in their one-room cabins to tell stories and to pray that one day freedom would be theirs.

Some refused to wait for that distant hope of freedom. They escaped in the night, silently leaving the slave quarters as the master's "big house" loomed behind them in the dark. All night, they followed the stars to the north. During the day, they hid in the forests. Some made their way to "safe houses"—homes of people who devoted themselves to helping slaves gain

LINCOLN'S HEROES: HENRY CLAY and DEWITT CLINTON

Today, we look up to Lincoln as one of our country's greatest leaders. Lincoln had heroes too, and Henry Clay was one of them. Born during the American Revolution, Clay grew up to help negotiate peace between America and Britain. He was a Kentucky slaveholder who worked to abolish slavery. He was charming and hotheaded; he was nicknamed both "the Great Compromiser" and "the Dictator." He was criticized from all sides during his time and yet is often called one of the greatest senators in U.S. history. Clay is best remembered for the Missouri Compromise, an act that kept the feuding states intact—at least for a time. He was intelligent, passionate, sympathetic to the views of others, and devoted to the Union. He spoke with a voice like a fine musical instrument.

Henry Clay

DeWitt Clinton

Young Abraham Lincoln worshipped Henry Clay and said he was the perfect statesman.

Lincoln also said he wanted to be the DeWitt Clinton of Illinois. Clinton held many offices, including Governor of New York. He founded the public school system of that state, worked for fair crime laws and the abolition of slavery, and was responsible for the creation of the Erie Canal. Born into a prestigious family, Clinton was bold, energetic, and very popular. When he sailed in the first boat to travel from Lake Erie to New York City, people lined up along the Erie Canal to see him. When he emptied a vial of Lake Erie water into the Atlantic Ocean, crowds cheered wildly. The canal—called "Clinton's Ditch"—made New York an important port city.

their freedom. These slaves were escaping on the "Underground Railroad," not an actual railroad but a network of routes to the North. Sometimes a "conductor" drove them to the next safe house hidden inside the false bottom of a wagon. They found their destinations by secret signs, such as a lantern in a certain window, or a "safe quilt," with special messages sewn into it, hanging over a porch.

Slaves could be beaten or even killed for running away. Trackers pursued fugitives through the woods, across rivers, and over state lines to capture and return them to their masters. Some runaways made it all the way to Canada

Slave auction ❖ Library of Congress

and freedom. Some stayed in Northern states or in cities like New Orleans, trying to blend in with free blacks and make new lives with forged identities. Even in free states, life was not easy. Blacks in Illinois could not vote, sit on juries, or attend school. Racism was common and opportunities few. Even free blacks were sometimes captured by corrupt trackers and brought to slave states and sold.

Other slaves revolted. One group tried to take over the Richmond, Virginia, armory. Another plotted to wage war against slave owners in Charleston, South Carolina. Their leaders were captured and executed. In a Louisiana revolt, 66 slaves were killed. In the same year that Abraham Lincoln took a flatboat downstream for the second time, Virginia slave Nat Turner, along with six others, killed his master and others at nearby plantations and attracted a small army of slaves to his rebellion. Turner was caught and hanged; 60 whites and more than 100 blacks were killed during the uprising.

Earlier in that same year, a Massachusetts man, William Lloyd Garrison, started a newspaper dedicated to ending slavery. He called it *The Liberator.* Garrison was part of a group of antislavery people known as "abolitionists." "I WILL BE HEARD!" he claimed, promising he would not back down an inch until slavery was abolished. Garrison and other abolitionists wrote articles, made speeches, handed out pamphlets, and urged politicians to end slavery.

A lot of people didn't like abolitionists—even people who didn't like slavery themselves—because they thought abolitionists were troublemakers, meddling in things that were none of their business. Many Southerners blamed the abolitionists for slave uprisings. Many Northerners were prejudiced against blacks. They didn't want freed slaves moving to their states. There were people who thought it was best just to leave the whole thing alone, in order to keep peace between the Northern and Southern states. Others thought slavery

William Lloyd Garrison

CONDUCTORS ON THE UNDERGROUND RAILROAD

It was **illegal** to help runaway slaves, and those who did risked fines and imprisonment. But in spite of the risks, more than 3,200 people worked on the Underground Railroad.

Levi and Catharine Coffin were Quakers who sheltered 3,000 fugitive slaves in their home, later known as the "Grand Central Station of the Underground Railroad." Levi was nicknamed the railroad's "president."

Though born to a rich Virginia slave-holding family, **John Fairfield** found imaginative ways to bring slaves to the North. He once had a slave play dead in a coffin and told 27 others to pretend to be a grieving funeral procession—which marched its way to freedom.

In Philadelphia, **William Still**, son of former slaves, took in thousands of fugitive slaves. One day he opened his door to a fugitive who was his own brother. Another day, Still received a wooden packing box labeled "This Side Up." The box contained a slave named Henry Brown (Henry was forever after known as "Box" Brown). William Still later wrote a book about the Underground Railroad.

Harriet Tubman, herself an escaped slave, rescued her sister from the auction block, then went back south 19 times to lead more than 200 other slaves out of bondage. Angry slave owners offered thousands of dollars for her capture but they never caught her—and, she said, "I never lost a passenger."

would eventually become unprofitable and just fade away, so why make a fuss?

After selling his goods, Abraham spent a month in New Orleans before returning home. With its elegant brick homes and noisy streets, New Orleans was an exciting place for a young frontiersman. It was one of the busiest port cities in the United States. Steamboats lined the river's banks; roustabouts (men who worked on the waterfront) loaded and unloaded their cargo. In charming boutiques, finely dressed ladies fingered laces and silks. Traders bartered, in English and French, in the cotton, sugar, and slave markets. Abraham saw a wider world, and had plenty to think about on his return home. He bought passage on a steamboat to St. Louis and walked from there across Illinois to his father's home. Remembering Denton Offutt's promise of a job, he made his way to New Salem. There, Offutt offered him a position in his general store, and a place to sleep in the back.

Abraham's boss was so pleased with his new employee that he told everyone who came through the village about the fine young man who clerked at his store. He was smart as a whip and strong as an ox. He was capable, bright, and honest in his business dealings and able to lift heavy boxes and barrels as if they were feather-light. In an era when the average man's height was five feet, six inches tall, Abraham towered at six foot four. He was so big and strong, said the trader, that young Abe could whup anyone in town or out of it.

Abraham might have been happier if his boss had kept quiet. He enjoyed the footraces and jumping contests held on the dusty New Salem roads (and with his long legs, found it easy to win them). But he never liked fistfights and wrestling bouts, in which rowdy men pulled hair and gouged eyes. When a rough gang called the Clary's Grove Boys heard about Abraham's reputation as a strong man, they challenged him to a wrestling match with their leader, the brawny Jack Armstrong. Abraham had to fight.

The opponents faced each other with coats off and sleeves rolled up. Men shouted them on, betting among themselves for their favorite. Later, people told stories about the fight, and the details got blurred. Some said Lincoln won fair and square and others said Armstrong won (but cheated). Onlookers said that Armstrong's men, angry that Abraham got the best of their Jack, were eager to spring on him. Abraham offered to take them all on, one at a time. Impressed by his courage, the Clary's Grove Boys befriended the newcomer. He won their loyalty and the friendship of Jack Armstrong.

Abraham told his neighbors he had landed in New Salem like "a piece of floating driftwood," but he made friends easily and began to feel at home. People came to the store to buy and stayed to hear the clerk's stories and jokes. They liked the tall young man with the bushy black hair. He soon knew the 100 residents of the little village, as well as settlers from outlying communities who came to trade at the general store.

With its mills, workshops, inn, stores, school, and two doctors, New Salem was a bustling center of activity. The blacksmith labored in his sweltering shop; the hatter boiled felt in a kettle outside his door; the cooper crafted barrels, buckets, and tubs. Farmers drove wagonloads of grain to the mill or brought their horses to the smithy to be fitted with horseshoes. Women wove baskets, made soap, and tended vegetable gardens. Travelers stayed at the Rutledge Tavern, where a hot meal and an overnight stay cost them less than 40 cents. On Sundays, people gathered at the schoolhouse to hear rousing sermons, then stayed in town to gossip with neighbors or watch wrestling matches and shooting contests.

Abraham slept at the store or roomed with different New Salem families. Jack Armstrong's wife, Hannah, was always glad to see him. Abraham brought candy for the children and rocked the baby's cradle while Hannah did chores. She mended his clothes and listened to his thoughts. "He was always at home wherever he went," said another neighbor, and he generally had a laughing child hanging on him.

Abraham was glad to have found a place in the world, but he was still not satisfied. He was hungry for knowledge and determined to excel. He felt it was important to speak correctly, so when he heard that a neighbor owned a grammar book he walked six miles to the man's house to borrow it. During slow hours

New Salem, Illinois ❖ Tim Ross

at the store, he stretched out on the counter to study. He taught himself mathematics too, scratching out problems on scraps of paper. He talked about books with Mentor Graham, the local schoolmaster, and learned poetry and the works of Shakespeare from an educated neighbor. Wanting to challenge himself, he showed up at the local debating club and asked to give a speech. His listeners settled in, expecting one of Abraham's humorous stories. Instead the nervous young man stood before them, hands in his pockets, and gave a well-reasoned and serious lecture. Innkeeper James Rutledge recalled that "all were amazed."

When the local court was in session, Abraham eagerly attended. In those days, watching trials on "court days" was considered great entertainment. There were no courthouses in the small communities, so judges heard trials in their own cabins or in large tavern rooms. Juries—made up of hunters dressed in breeches and farmers in homespun—sat on rough log benches. Spectators heard trials about assaults and land claims, prairie burnings, and, rarely, murder.

The judge of the local court, a stout man named Bowling Green, liked Abraham Lincoln and encouraged him to comment on cases. At times the young man's arguments were so amusing that Green's sides shook with laughter. But Abraham's arguments were also thoughtful and interesting, and the judge became more and more impressed with his good sense and good mind. Abraham's neighbors were impressed, too, and asked him to draft

THINK LIKE LINCOLN

One of the most amazing things about Abraham Lincoln was his great intellect. Because he never stopped exercising his mind, his lack of schooling did not hold him back. He studied geometry, trigonometry, and the works of Shakespeare. As president, he taught himself military science.

One man who knew him well said that Lincoln never forgot a thing he heard or read. He had great powers of concentration and a "thoughtful and investigating mind which dug down after ideas, and never stopped till the bottom facts were reached." His stepmother said he needed to understand everything "minutely and exactly" and would repeat things over to himself until they were fixed in his mind. How can you think like Lincoln?

- When you really want to learn something, read it out loud. (Lincoln often did; as he put it, two senses are better than one.)
- Learn a new word every day and memorize a new poem every month.
- After you learn something, write it down in your own words.
- Do crossword puzzles and word jumbles. Play games like chess.
- Challenge your mind by challenging your body—learn a complicated dance step or other physical activity that is new to you.
- Play complex and stimulating music (like Mozart).
- Learn a foreign language.
- Take up a new and challenging hobby.

deeds and other legal papers for them. Perhaps his neighbors' confidence in his abilities made him think he could do more. Abraham decided to run for political office.

Just as Abraham announced his ambition for the state legislature, Illinois's governor put out a call for volunteer soldiers. Sauk Indian chief Black Hawk had crossed the Mississippi River, and settlers feared for their lives. The Sauk and Fox tribes had moved to Iowa as white settlers came west, but they had suffered sickness and hunger there. They wanted to return to their tribal lands in Illinois to plant corn. When Chief Black Hawk and his people, including 500 warriors, entered Illinois, villagers and settlers across the prairies panicked. Black Hawk had once set fire to a settlement—who knew what he intended now? In one town, a false alarm sent hundreds of people flying to a fort, with babies screaming and sick people dragged from their beds. Women feared capture; men feared scalping. Young men, including Abraham, signed up to fight.

"To his own surprise," Lincoln said, he was elected captain of his company: as men lined up behind the possible captain of their choice, Lincoln's line grew longer and longer until he got a unanimous vote. (Years later, after many accomplishments, he said that this success "gave me more pleasure than any I have had since.")

"I AM YOUNG AND UNKNOWN TO MANY OF YOU."

After less than a year in New Salem, when he was only 23, Abraham decided to become a candidate for Illinois's state legislature. It might seem odd to us today that this young man, who had no political experience and almost no schooling, would run for office. It probably didn't seem so odd to him or his neighbors. Settlers had broken the wild lands and built thriving communities. Though just ordinary people, they felt confident in their ability to take care of, and govern, themselves. Who better than ordinary settlers to make decisions about their own community?

Today, politicians might seem like powerful figures who make decisions for us, but the role of government is to serve its people. Ordinary people do and should run for office. Ordinary people should make their voices heard by those who enact our laws.

"I am young and unknown to many of you," Abraham wrote in his campaign announcement. He outlined his hopes to serve his community by working for improvements in education and river transportation. He closed saying, "I have no [ambition] so great as that of being truly esteemed by my fellow men, by rendering myself worthy of their esteem."

As captain of this rough company, which included the Clary's Grove Boys, Lincoln had his hands full commanding discipline. "Go to the devil, sir!" one shouted when Captain Lincoln gave his first order. He had to threaten his men when they wanted to kill an innocent, aged Indian who wandered into their camp

CHIEF BLACK HAWK was taken prisoner and toured around the United States so he could see firsthand the power of the white government. To his surprise, crowds in the eastern cities cheered him as a hero. They saw him as a symbol of courage and of the wild frontier. He sat for a portrait and told his story to a translator. Years later, sculptor Lorado Taft created a 50-foot-tall statue of the chief. It stands today above the Rock River in Illinois. You can make a statue of Chief Black Hawk, too.

WHAT YOU NEED

- Newspaper
- Toilet paper roll
- Masking tape
- Bowl
- ½ cup white glue
- ½ cup water
- Stirring stick
- Black or red pipe cleaner
- Brown paper (a paper bag will work)
- Scissors
- White glue
- Tempera paints
- Paint brushes

Cover your workspace with newspaper. For the body of the statue, ball up a piece of newspaper and stuff it into an end of the paper roll. Tape together. Make a smaller ball for the head and tape it on top. Roll small pieces of newspaper to make arms. Place them so they are folded in front of the body and tape.

In a bowl, stir glue and water together. Rip several sheets of newspaper into long strips ½ to 1 inch wide. Dip a strip in the glue mixture. Hold it at one end. With your other hand, press your fingers along the length of the strip, top to bottom, to squeeze off excess liquid. Wrap the strip around the figure. Repeat until the figure is covered with two layers of strips. Let dry for 24 hours.

Construct nose, chin, and ears using small bits of newspaper dipped in the glue mixture. Add another layer of strips, then let dry again overnight.

Paint the statue. Wet and wring out the brown paper, let it dry, and cut to create a cloak. Fold the collar down and snip along its edge to make fringe. Place over Black Hawk's shoulders. Glue a small piece of pipe cleaner down the middle of the head to make Black Hawk's headpiece.

one night. "Choose your weapons," he said, challenging them to fight their own captain if they harmed the old man. Learning drills was another challenge. When marching his men, 20 across, over a field, he forgot the command that would narrow the line to get them through a gate. "Halt!" he shouted, then ordered his company to break ranks for two minutes and form again on the other side of the gate.

Lincoln later made light of his experiences during the Black Hawk War, saying he had fought no battles but "had a good many bloody struggles with mosquitoes." But it was no easy time. He and his men pursued

Chief Black Hawk

Black Hawk's band into Wisconsin, marching through swamps and pathless, brushy forests. They went hungry and slept in the rain. They saw scalped, disfigured soldiers left on battlefields. One morning, as sunlight painted the landscape blood red, Lincoln buried five men who had been killed and scalped. When his 30-day enlistment ended, Lincoln signed up again, then once more. When Black Hawk surrendered, Lincoln's soldiering came to an end. He walked and canoed, a four-day journey, back to New Salem.

Back home, Lincoln had only days to campaign for the state legislature. He ran as a member of the Whig party. He traveled around the county, making stump speeches in small villages. One man who saw him said Lincoln was gawky and rough looking, wearing a straw hat, with one suspender holding up pants that "didn't meet his shoes by six inches." But after Lincoln started to speak, his thoughtfulness "made a considerable impression" on all. At one campaign stop, he made a different kind of impression. When a fight broke out in the crowd while Lincoln was speaking, he rushed over, picked the attacker up by the neck and threw him 12 feet.

Lincoln lost his campaign for the state legislature and, when Offutt's store closed down, found himself without a job. He and a friend jumped at the chance to buy out one of the

"My politics are short and sweet, like the old woman's dance."

—Abraham Lincoln during his first campaign for office

"Lincoln the Campaigner" ❖ Indiana Historical Society

WHAT IN THE WORLD
IS A WHIG?

Political parties are organizations made up of people who share similar ideas about government. They develop platforms (positions) that outline their party's goals, and choose candidates for political office.

Young Abraham Lincoln belonged to the Whig Party. Whigs thought President Andrew Jackson had become far too powerful (they called him "King Andrew"). They stood for a regulated economy and thought the government should create roads, canals, and railroads. They borrowed the name "Whig" from early American patriots who fought for freedom from Britain's King George III.

Other parties during Lincoln's lifetime included the Democrats and Republicans, the Free-Soilers, and the Know-Nothings. (The members of this last party, formed to prevent immigration, liked to keep things secret; when asked a question about their party, they replied "I know nothing!")

In simple terms, today's Republican Party tends to support business and industry and to oppose government spending on social programs. Democrats generally believe the federal government should play a more active role in overseeing industry and in supporting social programs. In earlier times, these parties stood for other issues.

There are other parties—like the Reform Party (which promotes ethical standards in government) and the Green Party (which supports environmental issues)—but for over 150 years, American presidents have been either Democrats or Republicans. These parties have become so powerful that our political process hinges on the two-party system. Will it always? Will you join a party or start one of your own?

other general stores in New Salem. But after a time, as Lincoln put it, their business venture "winked out." (This partnership left Lincoln burdened with bills, which he jokingly called "the national debt." It would take him 15 long years to repay his creditors.) Lincoln turned again to the useful ax and earned his keep chopping trees, clearing land, and splitting rails. He nearly decided to become a blacksmith, then was delighted when he got a job as New Salem's postmaster. This job allowed him to read all the newspapers delivered to New Salem and to chat with neighbors when they came to pick up their mail. If they didn't come by, the young postmaster put their letters in his cap and delivered them.

A new opportunity—the prospect of becoming a surveyor—sent Lincoln off to borrow more books. He stayed up nights with schoolmaster Mentor Graham, learning the geometry and trigonometry he needed for this job. After he mastered the required knowledge, he shouldered his surveyor's compass, chain, and staff and set out for the countryside.

As a surveyor, Lincoln plotted routes for roads, boundaries of farms, and even plans for new towns on the prairie. Often, when people disagreed about property boundaries, they called on Lincoln to settle the dispute. He traveled on horseback, meeting new people in the budding communities. These new acquaintances remembered the friendly young man when he ran for political office again. Some teased him into harvesting a field, saying they couldn't vote for a man unless he showed himself to be a hard worker. "Boys," he said, taking a turn in the field, "if that is all, I am sure of your votes." His hard work paid off; in his second campaign, Lincoln was elected to the Illinois House of Representatives.

Lincoln had learned to soldier and to survey. Now that he was to be a state legislator, he needed to learn the law. John Todd Stuart, a fellow legislator and a friend from the Black Hawk War, urged Lincoln to become a lawyer and lent him some law books to study. New Salem's residents were amused to see Lincoln reading while he walked, or standing in the middle of the road with his face in a book. He spent whole days reading beneath a tree, moving only enough to stay in the shade. Then, when the legislative session was about to begin, Lincoln borrowed money from a friend, bought a new suit of clothes, and boarded a stagecoach bound for the state capital.

[LEFT] *Berry-Lincoln Store, New Salem* ❖ Tim Ross

[ABOVE] *Abraham Lincoln, "Deputy Surveyor"*
❖ Tim Ross

SURVEYOR LINCOLN used a compass for direction, a heavy chain to measure land, and trigonometry to calculate angles and distances. You can leave the hard math for high school and just have some fun! Use surveying techniques to create a puzzle for treasure seekers. It will lead them from a starting point along several segments to the treasure. Learn real surveying terms (the words in italics) in the definitions to the right.

WHAT YOU NEED

- ⊠ 5 or more friends (a surveyor, a rodman, a chainman, and some treasure seekers)
- ⊠ Measuring tape
- ⊠ Pencil
- ⊠ Heavy string, 25 feet long
- ⊠ 2 long, straight sticks, about chest high
- ⊠ File folder labels
- ⊠ Black marker
- ⊠ Compass
- ⊠ 1 flat rock
- ⊠ Treasure
- ⊠ Logbook

Make a surveyor's *chain* by measuring 10 inches from one end of the heavy string. Fold a file folder label over the string so it adheres to itself at that spot. Mark "Link 1" on the label. Measure another 10 inches from that spot,

SURVEYING TERMS

Bearing: Line of direction (north, south, east, west, etc.).

Benchmark: A survey mark that serves as a reference point.

Chain/Chainman: Surveyors measured with iron chains made up of 100 links (each link 7.92 inches long). A square the length of one chain on each side measured off an acre. Sturdy chainmen dragged the 66-foot chains through swamps and dense forests.

Jacob's staff: A long rod used to mount and steady the compass.

Landmark: A permanent feature like a tree or a rock.

Point of beginning: The starting point for a survey.

Rod/Rodman: Surveyors sighted toward a 10-foot pole, or a rod, held by an assistant called a rodman.

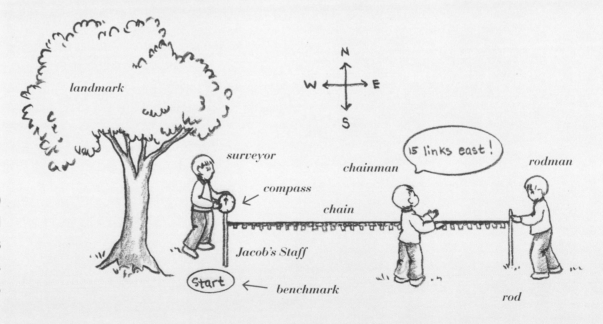

attach another label, and mark it "Link 2." Continue until you have 30 links.

Choose a *landmark*, like a tree or the corner of your house, in a park or your backyard. Write "Start" on the flat rock and place it at the landmark. This *benchmark* will be the *point of beginning* for your survey and treasure hunt. Note the benchmark's location in your logbook.

The surveyor should place one stick (called a *Jacob's staff*) on top of the benchmark. Place the compass on top of the staff, hold it steady until the needle settles, and turn the compass's dial to align North with the needle's direction. Choose the direction (N, S, E, W) you'd like for the first segment. Direct the *rodman* to take the other long stick (the *rod*) to a distant point in that direction and place the rod in the ground. You can guide the rodman there by sighting along the lines on the compass and having him or her move left or right until the rod lines up precisely along the line you're sighting. Ask a *chainman* to walk one end of the chain to the rod while you hold the other end at the benchmark. The chain should be held tight and waist high. Have the chainman shout out the number of links so that the surveyor can record the direction (or *bearing*) and the number of links in the logbook.

The surveyor now joins the rodman and replaces the rod with the Jacob's Staff. Choose a new direction and repeat the process, noting the direction and number of links each time. At the last spot, leave the treasure.

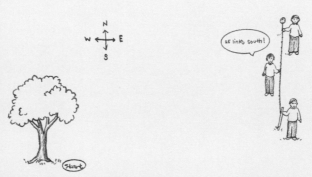

The notes in your logbook should look something like this:

Benchmark	Maple tree
Segment 1	15 Links East
Segment 2	12 Links Northeast
Segment 3	25 Links South
Segment 4	8 Links West (look for treasure)

Give the logbook, compass, and chain to the treasure-seekers. See if they can follow the lines of your survey to reach the treasure!

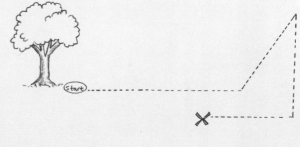

"THE LONG AND SHORT OF IT"

Abraham Lincoln's political career began modestly in Illinois's modest capital, Vandalia. During his first months in its shabby statehouse, Lincoln quietly watched and learned. He and the other legislators sat at long tables, debating projects and issues while chunks of plaster fell from the ceiling. Legislative sessions lasted months. In between them, Lincoln returned to New Salem, where he studied law books and "mixed in surveying work" to pay his bills. In time, he grew more comfortable with his new role and stepped up to support a state bank and transportation improvements.

Reelected, he became known as the longest of the "Long Nine," a group of legislators who were each so tall their combined height added up to 54 feet. The Long Nine worked to have the state capital moved to the town of Springfield. New settlers had shifted the population to the north and it made sense for the state's government to be at a more central site.

Illinois was no longer a frontier land. People had poured in from states east, north, and south, from Ireland, Great Britain, and Germany. Towns grew, roads and bridges were built, steamboats plied the rivers, and soon railroads would connect small towns across the state. Lincoln supported these improvements by voting for railroads and the Illinois and Michigan Canal, a project that would connect Lake Michigan to the Mississippi River.

During his four terms in the Illinois legislature, Lincoln became a leader of the Whig party and was even nominated by his party for a position as Speaker of the House. His reputation had grown. It suffered a little over something he later called "that jumping scrape." He and his fellow Whigs had hoped to prevent a quorum from meeting in order to delay an important vote. (A quorum is the minimum number of members necessary for a vote to be taken.) When enough members of the opposing party showed up at the statehouse to make a quorum, Lincoln and his friends tried to bolt out the door. Their rivals held it shut. He and two other Whigs then jumped out the second-story window! A newspaper article joked that the jump didn't hurt Lincoln at all, because his long legs "reached nearly from the window to the ground." It suggested that a third-floor meeting room might make members think twice about trying such an escape.

After years of studying on his own, Lincoln became a lawyer. His friend John Todd Stuart offered him a position in his busy Springfield law office. Lincoln packed his few books and belongings and said good-bye to his New Salem friends. His borrowed horse picked its way through Springfield's muddy streets while he looked over the new and booming town. It had hotels and stores, churches and schools, even a newspaper! Where would he fit in?

"I am quite as lonesome here as I ever was anywhere in my life," Lincoln wrote a friend weeks later. "I have been spoken to by but one woman since I've been here, and should not have been by her, if she could have avoided it." But he wasn't lonely for long.

Work kept him busy. He was still in the legislature, which met in a Springfield church until a new statehouse could be built. He wrote legal documents in Stuart's office and represented clients in the courtroom downstairs and in courts in nearby counties. Stuart put him in charge of keeping the office accounts, which Lincoln did badly. He stuffed important papers in his pockets or in his new, tall stovepipe hat. Still, Stuart had enough confidence in his young partner to leave Lincoln in charge when Stuart left for Washington to serve in Congress.

Lincoln found a friend and a place to stay when he shopped at Joshua Speed's general store. His goods came to a total of $17—much more than he had to spend. Speed later said he'd never seen so "gloomy and melancholy a face" as Lincoln's when the young lawyer explained he was short of funds. Speed came up with a plan that would save Lincoln money. "You are perfectly welcome to share a room with me," he said. When Lincoln heard that the room was right above the store, he collected his bags, went up the stairs, and came back down smiling. "Well, Speed," he said, "I'm moved!"

Joshua Speed, who had also been born in Kentucky, became one of Lincoln's closest friends. Young William Herndon, who clerked at the store and also slept in the crowded upstairs room, became another. Speed's store was a favorite gathering place and soon, according to Herndon, the young men who met there started a club for "debate and literary efforts." They read each other's poems and argued about politics while warming themselves by the fireplace in the back of Speed's store.

There was plenty for the young men to argue about. There was the current economic crisis, then the presidential election between Van Buren and Harrison, and, always, slavery. With the abolition movement growing stronger, arguments about slavery were heard across the country. Friends, families, and churches split over the issue. Communities were torn by riots and lynchings. Abolitionists—blamed for

Springfield, Illinois ❖ North Wind Picture Archives

LINCOLN AT THE LYCEUM

Imagine a time before movies or television, a time when even books were hard to get. What did people do for entertainment? When Abraham Lincoln was young, lyceums were popular. These were associations that hosted lectures and debates. Springfield's Young Men's Lyceum drew crowds. They heard lectures on topics like blood circulation and geology. One lecture even addressed the question "Who is happier—married or single people?"

A speech Lincoln gave at Springfield's Lyceum was published in the local newspaper. In it, he said that Revolutionary War heroes had fought passionately to gain America's freedom but that the time for passion was over. He warned against emotion in politics. The United States was "an undecided experiment," Lincoln said, and when vicious people "throw printing presses into rivers and shoot editors . . . this Government cannot last."

Lincoln was referring to abolitionist Elijah P. Lovejoy, a printer who had been calling for the end of slavery in his Alton, Illinois, newspaper. Twice, an angry crowd destroyed his printing presses. During a third attack, Lovejoy was killed. News of his death spread across the nation. Many called the tragedy an attack on freedom of speech and Lovejoy a martyr to abolitionism.

Lincoln asked his audience to set emotion aside and be guided by reason and respect for the Constitution. "Reverence for the law," he said, should become "the political religion of the nation."

Proslavery rioters burn the print shop of Elijah Lovejoy. ❧ North Wind Picture Archives

inciting slave revolts—received death threats. "End slavery now!" cried some people. "End it and the Union dies!" replied others. In the South, talk of secession (breaking away from the Union) grew louder. "The federal government has no right to interfere!"

For the moment, the federal government showed no interest in interfering with slavery. For years, the House of Representatives had had "gag rules" which said congressmen couldn't even discuss antislavery petitions. So many people were uncomfortable with the way that abolitionists "riled things up" that some Northern states, including Illinois, answered the appeals of Southern state governments by officially denouncing abolitionist societies. Only a handful of legislators, including Abraham Lincoln, protested. He and a colleague said they believed that "the institution [of slavery] is founded on both injustice and bad policy."

One of the young men who warmed himself at Speed's store was Stephen A. Douglas, a feisty, intelligent man who loved nothing more than a good argument. A prominent Democrat, he was called "the Little Giant" for his small size and his big role in Illinois politics. He and Lincoln agreed on very little, from the state bank to the presidential election. But they did agree that Mary Todd was one of the most charming ladies in town.

Mary Todd had come to Springfield from Kentucky to visit her sister and brother-in-law, Elizabeth and Ninian Edwards. Soon she was the belle of Springfield, and bachelors like Lincoln and Douglas were calling on her at the Edwardses' fine home.

This was not Lincoln's first courtship. His New Salem neighbors said he had once loved Ann, the daughter of New Salem tavern owner James Rutledge. Some even said they had been engaged. With her auburn hair, blue eyes, and kind nature, Ann could easily inspire romantic feelings. When she died young, probably of typhoid, people said Lincoln was devastated, almost crazy. The summer that Ann died was a rainy season; according to one friend, Lincoln said he couldn't bear the idea of the rain falling on Ann's grave.

Lincoln felt shy and unsure of himself around most women. He had begun a half-hearted courtship with a friend's sister, Mary Owens, when the friend hinted that she would bring Mary to New Salem if Lincoln would marry her. Lincoln had once seen Mary, and thought her pretty. "[I] saw no good objection to plodding through life hand in hand" with her, he said. After she arrived, he was sorry he had said it. For her part, Mary Owens said that Lincoln was "deficient in those little links which make up the chain of a woman's happiness." Lincoln was so tender-hearted he ruined his best clothes to rescue a hog mired in the mud, yet when he and Mary went riding he crossed a dangerous river without even looking back to see if she made it. Still, he felt honor-bound to keep his word and propose to her. To his surprise, she rejected him. "I have now come to the conclusion never again to think of marrying," he wrote a friend, "and for this reason; I can never be satisfied with any one who would be block-head enough to have me."

Mary Todd changed his mind. She was small and plump with chestnut hair and sparkling blue eyes. She was witty, intelligent, and cultured. They had much in common. They were both from Kentucky and each had lost a mother at an early age. They shared a passion

Abraham Lincoln; Mary Todd Lincoln ❖ Library of Congress

"I am destined to marry a president."

—Mary Todd, as a young girl

for poetry and Whig politics. She even knew Lincoln's hero, Henry Clay, who was her father's friend.

In many ways, though, Lincoln and Mary Todd were entirely different. Lincoln came from the poorest background and had despised slavery as long as he could remember. Mary's father was a prestigious Kentucky banker and a slave owner. Mary, with her finishing school education, spoke French and charmed suitors on the dance floor. The self-taught Lincoln, with his messy hair and spindly legs, felt awkward in comparison. He towered over the petite Mary, who was only five feet tall (they were "the long and short of it," he liked to say). But he was smitten, according to Mary's sister Elizabeth, and would "listen and gaze on her as if drawn by some superior power." After a year of courtship, they agreed to marry.

Once they became engaged, Lincoln had doubts. Mary's sister thought Lincoln an honest and sincere man but felt the two were not well suited. He wondered if he could possibly make a happy life for Mary, who loved fine things and came from such an aristocratic family (one *d*, he said, was enough for God but the Todds needed two).

They broke their engagement and Lincoln was miserable. "If what I feel were equally distributed to the whole human family," he wrote a friend, "there would not be one cheerful face on the earth." Springfield gossips said Lincoln was suffering "two Cat fits and a Duck fit" and had gone as "crazy as a loon." His friend Joshua Speed, who had moved to Kentucky, invited Lincoln to his family's country home for some rest and quiet.

A friend brought Mary Todd and Lincoln back together, inviting each to her home and urging them to be friends. Soon, their courtship began again—but secretly this time, away

The Todd home in Lexington, Kentucky
❖ Jeff Herbert

from prying eyes and disapproving families. In the meantime, Lincoln's partnership with Stuart had dissolved. Lincoln had become a partner in Stephen T. Logan's law office and was serving his last term in the Illinois legislature.

One rainy November evening, in the parlor of her sister's home, Lincoln and Mary Todd married. They made their first home in a rented room at Springfield's Globe Tavern. Days later, Lincoln wrote a friend, "Nothing new here, except my marrying, which to me, is a matter of profound wonder."

Lincoln had come a long way from his childhood. He was a lawyer, a husband, and soon to be a father. The year after his marriage, son Robert Todd Lincoln was born. The year after that, the Lincolns bought a home, a plain house on a corner lot, with upstairs ceilings so low Lincoln couldn't stand up straight. With a well for water and a stable in back for their horse and cow, they had everything they needed. Months later, Lincoln started his own law practice and asked his friend William Herndon to join him as junior partner.

The Lincoln-Herndon Law Offices were a mess! Neither man liked to keep order. Books and papers were everywhere—in boxes, on desks, in piles on the floor. A pile on Lincoln's desk had a note on top saying "When you can't find it anywhere else, look in this." Lincoln still had a habit of putting papers in his hat,

EN GARDE!

"**C**avalry broadswords of the largest size. A plank 10 feet long which neither is to pass his foot over upon forfeit of his life. Thursday evening at 4:00. Within three miles of Alton, on the opposite side of the river." These were the terms of a duel between Abraham Lincoln and political opponent James Shields.

The quarrel between the two men started as a prank. Letters appeared in the Springfield newspaper, signed by a country woman named "Rebecca." She had a lot to say about politicians (that with the current set in office, she soon wouldn't have a cow left to milk) and especially about state auditor James Shields (that he never told the truth or even "a good, bright, passable lie"). The letters had a good many people in Springfield laughing, but James Shields didn't like them one bit.

"Rebecca" was actually Lincoln, Mary Todd, and her friend Julia. When Shields found out Lincoln was behind the insulting letters, he challenged him to a duel. According to the long-held customs of dueling code, Lincoln was allowed to choose the weapons. He chose swords. He had no intention of hurting Shields and thought that, with his long arms, he could stay far away from his opponent and remain unhurt himself.

Both of the men and their seconds (assistants) took a coach to Alton for the duel. Just as they were about to begin, friends showed up and put a stop to the fight. Lincoln was embarrassed about the entire incident and realized he had taken the prank too far.

which his partner called "an extraordinary receptacle, his desk and memorandum book." They let dirt pile up in the corners and spat orange seeds on the floor. (One visitor even

ABRAHAM LINCOLN used his tall, black stovepipe hat like a filing cabinet, keeping important letters and papers inside. What will you keep inside this stovepipe hat?

WHAT YOU NEED

- Ruler
- 2 pieces of black poster board, 22 by 28 inches
- Pencil
- Scissors
- Paper clips
- Stapler
- Clear tape
- Black ribbon, 2 inches wide and 24 inches long
- Small envelope

Measure a 7-by-28-inch rectangle on one piece of poster board and mark it with a pencil. Cut it out. Wrap the rectangle around your head until it fits comfortably (a little extra room is good). Paper-clip the cylinder at the top and bottom to hold it then try it on again. When you're comfortable with the fit, staple the cylinder at the top and bottom.

Center the cylinder on the poster board. Slightly push in on two sides of the cylinder to make it an oval shape. Hold it down with one hand while trac-

ing an oval around the base with the other hand (or ask someone to help hold the cylinder while you trace). Remove the cylinder. Measure 1 inch out from the edge of the oval and draw another oval around the first one. Cut out along this outer oval. Cut slits from the outer oval approximately every 1 inch toward the inner oval to create tabs. Place the oval on top of the cylinder, folding the tabs inside to make a good fit. Turn the cylinder over, and tape the tabs to the inside of the cylinder.

To create the brim, place the cylinder over the remaining poster board. Hold it down with one hand while tracing an oval around the base with the other hand (this is oval A). Remove the cylinder. Measure 1½ inches out from the edge of oval A and draw another oval around it (this is oval B).

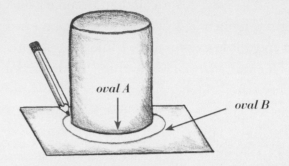

oval A

oval B

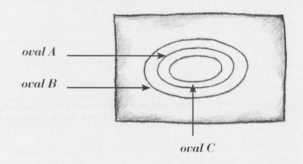

oval A

oval B

oval C

Measure 1 inch *in* from oval A and draw a third oval inside it (this is oval C). Cut around the outer oval (B), then cut along the inner oval (C). To make tabs, cut 1-inch slits from oval C to oval A.

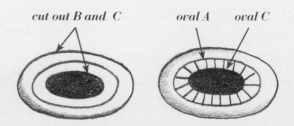

cut out B and C

oval A   oval C

With the cylinder covered end down, place this piece around the uncovered upper rim. Fold the tabs inside the cylinder and tape them in place.

Glue the ribbon around the base of the hat. To use your hat as a filing cabinet, cut the "v" off a small envelope, then tape the envelope to the inside of your hat. Use it to hold very important papers!

claimed that the seeds sprouted in the dirt!) But in spite of the mess, theirs was a successful partnership and one of Springfield's busiest firms.

Every spring and fall, Lincoln packed a bag, mounted his horse Old Tom, and set out across Illinois's countryside. In those days, circuit court judges traveled from one county seat to another, holding court in each place for days or weeks. To get business, lawyers "rode the circuit" too. Judge and lawyers traveled together over muddy spring roads and in the crisp autumn air. When they came to a river, the judge looked to long-legged Lincoln to find the best place to cross. They shared tavern rooms, two or three to a bed, with only the portly judge allowed a bed of his own. In the evenings, lawyers, judge, and locals sat by the fire to talk. With his gift for funny stories, Lincoln was often at the center of the crowd. His eyes sparkled when he told a joke, and he could hardly keep himself from smiling. When he got to the punch line, no one laughed harder than he did.

The inns were noisy and often not clean. As many as 20 men might share a room, sleeping on old quilts or straw. None of it bothered Lincoln much. He didn't care about comforts, about clothes or even food. One night, when an innkeeper had no bread or meat, Lincoln cheerily said, "Well, in the absence of anything

WHATEVER Lincoln couldn't fit into his hat went into a carpetbag. These handy satchels served as the suitcases, briefcases, and purses of the 1800s.

Adult supervision required

WHAT YOU NEED
- Scissors
- 1 yard upholstery fabric
- Measuring tape
- Pins
- Needle and thread
- ⅜-inch dowel, cut into two 18-inch pieces (ask an adult to cut the dowel)
- One large button
- Marker

Cut fabric into a 24-by-24-inch square. On two opposite edges of the square, pin ½ inch of fabric to the unpatterned side of the material and stitch down. Fold in half

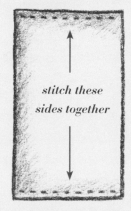

stitch these sides together

so the patterned side faces in and the stitched edges meet. The fabric piece is now shaped like a rectangle. Stitch each of the short sides of the rectangle together, ½ inch from their edge, to make a bag. Turn the bag inside out so the pattern is on the outside.

Cut four pieces out of the remaining fabric, each 8 by 5 inches. Take one of these pieces and fold one long edge toward the middle. Fold the other long edge to overlap the first so that the piece measures 2 inches across. Pin down, then stitch all three layers together. Repeat with all four pieces. These will serve as handles for the carpetbag.

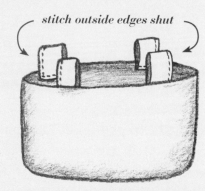

stitch outside edges shut

Fold one of the handles in half. Pin it to the inside of one side of the bag, 2 inches from one end, then stitch it on. Fold, pin, and stitch another handle 2 inches from the other end. Then fold, pin, and stitch the two remaining handles opposite the first two, on the other side of the bag (see illustration). Stitch the outside edges of each handle together. Place the dowels inside the handles. Stitch through the fabric as close to the dowels as possible, to help keep them in place.

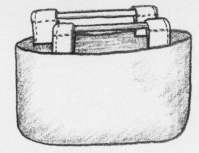

Cut a 5-by-5-inch piece from the remaining fabric. Fold and stitch as you did for the handles so that the piece is 5 inches long and 2 inches wide. Fold one of the short edges under ½ inch and stitch. Stitch the other short edge to the center of one side of the bag, on the inside. Sew the large button close to the edge on the opposite side of the bag from this piece. Fold the fabric piece over to close up the bag and meet the button. Use a marker to mark the place where the fabric piece meets the button. Cut through the fabric at that spot, creating a buttonhole large enough for the button to go through.

else to eat I will jump into this cabbage!" All summer long, he wore a linen duster, stained and travel-worn. In the winter, he threw a shawl over his shoulders and fastened it with a safety pin. He wrapped a cord around his umbrella to keep it shut and carried his papers in a carpetbag. He was, said another lawyer, "the ungodliest figure I ever saw."

At each new town, the lawyers met with clients whose trials were about to be held. With his intelligence, knowledge of the law, and friendly courtroom presence, Lincoln was a popular choice among the people who needed help. Once more, by traveling around the country, he got to know people and talked to them about their concerns. A man who once rode with him on the circuit said Lincoln seemed to know all the people they ran into—and their horses, too.

While Lincoln traveled, Mary learned how to keep house. She had been brought up as the pampered daughter of a wealthy man, but she learned to cook and clean. A string of hired girls came to help with the chores, but none of them were ever quite good enough for the quick-tempered Mary. At times her temper was directed at Lincoln. *Must* he answer the door in his stocking feet? Could he *please* read sitting in a chair and not stretched out on the floor? The worst for Mary was when Lincoln went into one of his blue spells, staring off sorrowfully into space. Mary would go into a rage, Lincoln would leave the house until she calmed down, and the neighbors would talk and talk. Still, Mary adored her husband and said he was "her all." Lincoln loved his wife, and treated her kindly and tenderly. They had another baby and named him Edward Baker Lincoln.

The same year that little Eddy was born, Lincoln ran for office in the U.S. House of Representatives. His opponent in the election was a well-known preacher who called Lincoln "an infidel" because Lincoln didn't belong to a church. The accusation meant nothing to the people who knew the tall lawyer as an honest and upright man. They cast their vote for Lincoln.

While Lincoln ran for office, the United States went to war against Mexico. American settlers in Texas (which was once part of Mexico) had rebelled against the Mexican government, created the Republic of Texas, and had Texas admitted to the Union as

Lincoln on horseback, "On the Prairie," by Anna Hyatt Huntington ❖ Tim Ross

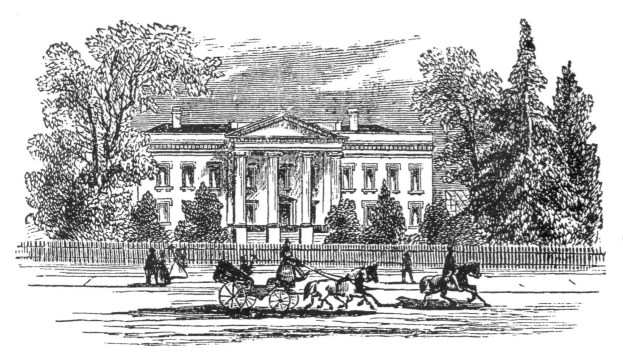

The White House

a slave state. Later, President James K. Polk ordered soldiers to the Rio Grande River. A skirmish broke out between American and Mexican soldiers over land claimed by both countries. Polk declared war.

As American soldiers marched to Mexico, the Lincoln family packed their belongings and moved to Washington. Mary tried to make a nice home in their modest boarding-house room, but she was lonely and unhappy, and the boys were restless. She moved with the children to her father's home in Lexington, Kentucky. Left alone, Lincoln wrote affectionate letters to his wife, sending his love to her and his "dear rascals." He studied nights at the Library of Congress or bowled with friends. He made friends with Alexander Stephens, a slight man from Georgia whose speeches brought tears to Lincoln's eyes.

Congressman Lincoln served on committees, answered petitions from his constituents, made speeches, and sent copies of them to the folks back home. Speaking in Congress, he wrote to Herndon, was just like speaking in court. "I was about as badly scared," he said, "and no worse." A newspaper praised one of Lincoln's speeches, saying, "He kept the House in a continuous roar of merriment." Another speech upset people and earned him the nickname of "Spotty Lincoln." In it, he called on the president to name the exact spot where the war had begun. President Polk claimed it was in United States territory but Lincoln believed Polk had lied about the spot in order to start a war. Speaking out against the war was considered unpatriotic. Lincoln was even called "traitorous" by an Illinois newspaper.

During his second year in Congress, Lincoln worked on a bill to end slavery in the District of Columbia, but his efforts came to nothing. He thought it was a terrible thing that slavery existed in the capital of a country dedicated to liberty. Lincoln proposed compensated emancipation for the slaves of Washington, D.C., meaning that their owners would be paid for the price of the freed slaves.

"Naturally anti-slavery," was how Lincoln described himself, saying, "I cannot remember when I did not so think, and feel." He wrote to a friend about having seen a group of "10 or a dozen slaves, shackled together with irons" on a trip along the Ohio River. "That sight was a continual torment to me," he said, "and I see something like it every time I touch the Ohio, or any other slave border."

In spite of that torment, Lincoln felt that the best way to end slavery was gradually. Pushing for the end of what Southerners called their "peculiar institution" created deep divisions between the two sections of the country. Lincoln thought that by working through the law to keep slavery restricted to those states where it already existed, it would die a natural death. Cotton crops exhausted the soil. Plantation

IN THE HEADLINES

Lincoln followed political events closely and read several newspapers every day. With new states forming and Southerners threatening to secede, there was excitement in the news.

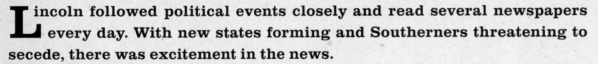

1848: Peace with Mexico! ∽ The peace treaty with Mexico brought vast new territories to the United States, including parts of present-day Arizona, California, Colorado, Nevada, New Mexico, Texas, and Utah.

1848: Gold! ∽ After gold was discovered in California, fortune-hunters raced to the West. American settlers there quickly applied for statehood.

1850: Compromise Reached! ∽ The Compromise of 1850 tried to please Southerners and Northerners alike. It admitted California as a free state, allowed the settlers of the New Mexico and Utah territories to decide for themselves about slavery, and banned the practice of selling slaves in the District of Columbia. A strong Fugitive Slave Act made capture more likely for escaped slaves.

1850: "Rough and Ready" Dies! ∽ When Mexican war hero and U.S. president Zachary Taylor died, Millard Fillmore became the new president.

1852: Mother of Six Writes Best-Seller! ∽ Harriet Beecher Stowe's *Uncle Tom's Cabin*, a moving story about the plight of slaves, sold 300,000 copies in its first year. It was read by everyone, including England's Queen Victoria. Southerners called the book abolitionist propaganda.

"How hard it is to die and leave one's country no better than if one had never lived for it."

—Abraham Lincoln to partner William Herndon

The Lincoln-Herndon Law Offices as a museum today ❖ Tim Ross

owners, in order to raise new crops, continually moved with their slaves to make plantations on new land. If they were restricted in where they could hold slaves, eventually, perhaps, they would give up on the institution.

During Lincoln's term in Congress, there were many angry arguments about slavery, especially about a bill called the Wilmot Proviso, which called for slavery to be excluded in any territory acquired from Mexico. Congressmen shouted and scuffled. Two of them even got into a fistfight! The bill was defeated.

When his term ended, Lincoln was offered the governorship of the Oregon Territory. He turned it down. Mary didn't like the idea of living in the wild western lands. Little Eddy was ill, and the move would be hard on him. The family settled back into their life in Springfield and Lincoln returned to his law office, sure that his political life had reached its end.

Lincoln and Herndon moved to a bigger (but no cleaner) office and their business grew, along with Lincoln's reputation as a masterful and honest lawyer. "Honest Abe," people called him. One judge thought so highly of him that when the judge was not available, he asked Lincoln to rule on the cases.

William Herndon also thought the world of his partner, but he got annoyed when Lincoln read out loud. He laughed at Lincoln's jokes, even when Lincoln told the same joke to two or three visitors in a row, but he rolled his eyes when Lincoln sprawled out on the couch, with his long legs over two chairs, to read the newspapers.

Herndon hated it when Lincoln's children came to the office to visit. The boys pushed papers on the floor, emptied inkstands, and danced on the mess. Lincoln, an indulgent parent, just laughed. He took them home, carrying them on his shoulders. His boys adored him, and the neighborhood children loved tall Mr. Lincoln too. When he appeared, they ran and jumped on him and knocked his hat off in play. He rewarded their pranks with cookies. He played marbles with the older boys, gave the little ones "horseback" rides, and took everyone to the circus.

The Lincolns cherished their children. They agonized when young Eddy got sick, and their hearts were broken when, after a long illness, he died. They welcomed a new baby, William Wallace, not long after. Two and a half years later, their youngest boy was born. They named him after Lincoln's father, Thomas, who had died a couple of years earlier. Young Thomas Lincoln looked like a tadpole, his father said, and the nickname "Tad" stuck.

Lincoln had been out of office for nearly five years and said he was "losing interest in poli-

A COURTROOM DRAMA

Attorney Lincoln took all kinds of cases and clients, from personal bankruptcy to patents to railroad business. One of his most famous cases involved the son of his old New Salem friend Jack Armstrong. Young "Duff" Armstrong was accused of murder. A witness said he clearly saw the attack at 11:00 P.M. on a bright, moonlit night. Lincoln asked the witness to tell the story again and again, inviting him to share every detail. The witness said there was no mistaking Duff's attack by the light of the full moon, which was high in the sky. Lincoln then pulled out an almanac showing that the moon had nearly set by the time the witness claimed the attack occurred. Duff Armstrong was found "not guilty."

tics." His business was thriving and his family settled into their life in Springfield. But one day he read a newspaper article describing the Kansas-Nebraska Act, a bill introduced in Congress by his old rival, now a senator, Stephen A. Douglas. This bill would repeal the Missouri Compromise, which outlawed slavery in the North. Instead, residents of Kansas and Nebraska would vote on whether their future states would be slave or free. Lincoln was shocked, stunned, and, finally, driven to act.

"THE RAIL SPLITTER FOR PRESIDENT!"

"We began by declaring that all men are created equal," Lincoln stated. "But now from that beginning we have run down to the other declaration, that for *some* men to enslave *others* is a 'sacred right of self-government.'" It was near the end of Lincoln's three-hour speech. In the audience, women waved handkerchiefs and men shouted as Lincoln scored points against his rival, Stephen A. Douglas, and Douglas's new law, the Kansas-Nebraska Act.

Lincoln captured his audience, speaking in a plain, straightforward fashion so that everyone could understand. He explained the history of the Louisiana Territory, the land that the United States had purchased from France back in President Jefferson's time. Some states had already been carved out of the territory. Settlers were now hoping to create two new states from it, Kansas and Nebraska. Lincoln explained how Congress had reached a compromise on what to do with the Louisiana Territory back when the people of Missouri

petitioned for statehood. Congress had agreed to allow Missouri into the Union as a slave state only if the rest of the Louisiana Territory would be free. Lincoln even quoted Douglas, who had once called the Missouri Compromise "a sacred thing which no ruthless hand would ever be reckless enough to disturb."

Lincoln next took his audience through the negotiations for peace with Mexico. New western lands had been added to the United States after the Mexican War. More compromises had been made concerning slavery in those lands. He then went back in time to talk about the men who had created the United States government. They never intended slavery to grow, he insisted. Yet now, with Nebraska and Kansas on the verge of statehood, this new Kansas-Nebraska Act could allow slavery into places where it was once outlawed.

Senator Douglas knew the Kansas-Nebraska Act would create trouble, but he thought it was worth it. As chairman of the Committee on Territories, he was eager to open up the western lands. Spanning the continent was considered America's "manifest destiny," but new states could not get accepted into the Union without long struggles in Congress. The arguments about whether or not slavery would be allowed in each new state slowed everything down. Douglas hoped the Kansas-Nebraska Act would solve those arguments by

IS IT FATE? THE IDEA OF MANIFEST DESTINY

When a journalist wrote that it was America's "manifest destiny to overspread the continent . . . for the development of the great experiment of liberty," many Americans agreed. They thought the expansion of the United States from sea to sea was inevitable (its "destiny") and so clear it was obvious ("manifest"). The United States grew with the annexation of Texas and the new lands gained in the Mexican War. But the expansion of slavery into new lands made many people question the idea of manifest destiny. Were they expanding liberty or spreading slavery? Use of the phrase—and belief in it—faded for a time, but got a new life in the 1890s, when it was used to promote U.S. overseas expansion.

taking the issue of slavery out of the hands of the federal government.

"Popular sovereignty" was the phrase Douglas used. It meant that the voters of the states would decide for themselves whether or not to have slavery. The United States government and its laws were designed so that some issues would be decided by the individual states. Other issues—like trade or making treaties with other countries—would be decided by the federal government. From Douglas's point of view, slaves were simply property, like a

THE LITTLE GIANT: STEPHEN A. DOUGLAS

When Lincoln first met Stephen A. Douglas, they were both young and ambitious politicians. But, Lincoln wrote, "With *me*, the race of ambition has been a failure—a flat failure; with *him* it has been one of splendid success."

Douglas was wealthy, famous, and one of Washington's most powerful senators. But when he first came to Illinois from New York he had been nearly penniless. He taught school, then opened a law practice, and soon was immersed in Illinois Democratic politics. He served as a state legislator, as Illinois secretary of state, and as justice on Illinois's supreme court; he was elected to the U.S. House of Representatives and the U.S. Senate.

Douglas was short and stocky, with a barrel chest, broad shoulders, and a big head made even bigger by a thick crown of hair. He chewed on cigars and waved his hands when he spoke. His deep voice carried far, so that everyone within earshot heard his strong opinions. He once so outraged an opponent that the man picked him up (Douglas bit him in the thumb). He believed in majority rule, states' rights, the expansion of the United States, and saving the Union.

SLAVERY AND CONGRESSIONAL COMPROMISES

The **Northwest Ordinance** (1787) ensured that states formed from territories north of the Ohio River and west to the Mississippi River would be free.

The Missouri Compromise (1820) balanced the number of slave and free states, accepted Missouri as a slave state, and outlawed slavery anywhere else in the Louisiana Territory north of the 36° 30′ latitude line.

The Compromise of 1850 admitted California as a free state, allowed the New Mexico and Utah territories to determine slave or free status, banned slave trade in the District of Columbia, and included a Fugitive Slave Act that strengthened laws against harboring runaway slaves and endangered free blacks and former slaves.

The Kansas-Nebraska Act (1854) overturned the Missouri Compromise, allowing voters in Kansas and Nebraska to vote on slave or free status.

cow or a horse, and not an issue for the federal government's authority. From Lincoln's point of view, slaves were human beings. "I would not trouble myself with the oyster laws of Virginia or the cranberry laws of Indiana," he said. But slavery was different. "Americans, south as well as north, shall we make no effort to arrest this?" he asked. Douglas sat in the front row of the audience, listening as Lincoln warned that if the Missouri Compromise was not restored, the Union might come to an end.

Though Lincoln did not hold any political office at that time, he felt the need to speak out. Soon he was back in the political fray, nominated once again for the state legislature. He won, but turned the office down when he was named as a candidate for a seat in the U.S. Senate. There, he felt, he could make a real difference in the direction his country was taking. He lost that campaign, felt the loss bitterly, and returned to his neglected law office to "pick up my lost crumbs."

In the meantime, one of the territories affected by the Kansas-Nebraska Act turned into a battleground. Nebraska was distant, with few settlers, but Kansas, right next to the slave state Missouri, was in the middle of a tug-of-war. "Free-soiler" and proslavery groups

"Stump Speaking in Early Bloomington," by Theophilus Adam Wylie ❧ Indiana University Archives

flooded the territory, each hoping to gain control of its new government. When Kansas territorial elections were held, proslavers from Missouri poured in, voted illegally, and gave Kansas a proslavery legislature. Bitter fights broke out. Neighbor rose up against neighbor. Antislavery "Kansas aid societies" from all over the country sent boxes of guns, labeling them "Beecher's Bibles" for a famous preacher who spoke out against slavery. Kansas received a nickname too—"Bleeding Kansas." A mob set fires in the town of Lawrence. Antislavery crusader John Brown led a midnight attack and slaughtered five proslavery settlers. Angry people retaliated with more shootings and burnings. The lynchings and massacres in Kansas took more than 200 lives.

Violence surfaced everywhere—even in the U.S. Senate. One day, a Southern congressman took his cane to an abolitionist senator and nearly beat him to death! Lincoln hated the brutality and violence. He warned his law partner against sending money for guns to Kansas. Herndon later said Lincoln told him instead to "revolutionize through the ballot box"—to speak up through his vote.

Across the country, people rose to action. Antislavery groups held rallies. The Republican Party, dedicated to keeping slavery out of the territories, was formed. They nominated explorer John Fremont for president. "Free

DIFFERENCES BETWEEN FRIENDS

Have you ever disagreed with a friend? Sometimes you can "agree to disagree" and still respect each other's opinions. Other times, when strong beliefs clash, it's hard to stay friends. You might have to decide which is more important, the thing you are fighting about or your friendship.

Lincoln's best friend, Springfield store owner Joshua Speed, had moved back to Kentucky, where he married, ran a farm, and owned slaves. Speed felt he would rather see the Union dissolved than give up his right to own slaves, which was guaranteed by the Constitution. Lincoln wanted the Union to stay together, even if it meant he had to set aside his feelings about slavery in the South. (But that didn't mean he wouldn't fight its extension to new territories!) "If for this you and I must differ, differ we must," he wrote Speed.

Before the introduction of the Kansas-Nebraska Act, the North and South had been able to maintain their relationship, even if they differed. But with the possibility of slavery's extension, everything changed. Many Northerners felt the act was the beginning of national slavery. White Southerners felt attacked by the North, and felt that their rights were about to be taken away. Most Southerners did not own slaves, but they did not want the federal government controlling them. They felt a greater allegiance to their state governments. Their cry became "states' rights!"

Lincoln tried to see the slavery issue from the Southern point of view. He thought that people were the same everywhere. He believed that if the South did not already have slavery, they would not introduce it. And if slavery existed in the North, "we should not instantly give it up."

Lincoln and Speed remained friends, in spite of their differences. But could the North and South remain a Union?

The Lincoln family home in Springfield, Illinois
❖ Tim Ross

rooms and raising the second floor. She had papered the walls in the latest patterns and hung heavy drapes over the windows. Their drawing room was as fancy as any in town. When Lincoln came home, he pretended he didn't recognize his own house. "Stranger," he said to a neighbor, "do you know where Lincoln lives? He used to live here."

One year later, Lincoln sat in the audience as Senator Douglas spoke. Everyone wanted to hear what Douglas would say about a recent Supreme Court decision. The case of *Scott v. Sandford* was about a slave, Dred Scott. Scott's master had moved from Missouri to live temporarily in Illinois and the Wisconsin territory, and he had brought his slave with him. In both of these places, slavery was against the law. Scott sued for his freedom, based on the fact that he had lived in free territory. His case worked its way up the court system until it was heard by the Supreme Court.

The Court decided against Dred Scott. Chief Justice Roger B. Taney declared that Dred Scott would remain a slave. He said slaves were not citizens and had no right to sue. Not only that, Taney said, but the Missouri Compromise was unconstitutional and Congress could not ban slavery in the western territories! Decades of government compromise on slavery came crashing down. The decision rocked the country.

soil, free speech and Fremont!" campaigners shouted. Lincoln, a lifelong Whig, joined the new party and gave a rousing speech at a Republican meeting. The Democrats nominated James Buchanan, a Northerner with Southern sympathies.

Lincoln spoke all over the state on behalf of his new party, but Buchanan won the presidency. Again, Lincoln returned to Springfield and his law office. Mary was glad to have him home. She had remodeled their house, adding

HOST A STRAWBERRY SOIREE!

ONCE MARY LINCOLN had her home fixed to her liking, she invited neighbors over for "sociables" and "strawberry parties." Strawberry parties were so popular in the 1850s that people said the country had "strawberry fever." Mary opened her parlor to their Springfield friends and served strawberries and cream to all.

Adult supervision required

WHAT YOU NEED

- Heavy white paper
- Red, green, and black markers
- Red and green construction paper
- Scissors
- White glue
- Envelopes
- Little baskets and strawberry plants
- White butcher paper
- Napkins, serving dishes, cups, plates, and utensils
- Ingredients for the following recipes

Write invitations with a red marker, asking your friends to wear their favorite red outfits to the party. Make tiny strawberries from construction paper and glue them onto the envelopes.

Make giant strawberries from construction paper (use the black marker to draw the seeds); use to decorate your door and the party room. Cover a table with white butcher paper and draw strawberry vines all over it. Write the party menu on a sheet of white paper, decorate it, and set it up on the table. Set out napkins, cups, plates, and utensils. Place strawberry plants in the baskets and set them around the room.

Follow the recipes below to make delicious strawberry treats. Right before your guests arrive, arrange the food on the table. Enjoy the strawberry soiree with your guests. Give each person a strawberry plant when he or she leaves.

PARTY GAMES

Pass the Strawberry: Line up and give each player a spoon. Then pass a strawberry down the line, spoon to spoon. See how far you can pass the berry without dropping it.

Strawberry Trivia: Read strawberry facts and "pretend facts" to your guests. See if they can guess which are true. (Some real strawberry facts: they are the only fruits with seeds on the outside; they are the first fruit to ripen in the spring; one billion pounds of strawberries are grown in California every year.)

RECIPES

Strawberry-Spinach Salad: Clean one 10-ounce bag of spinach and place in bowl. Add 3 sliced green onions and 1 pint of sliced strawberries. For dressing, mix 4 tablespoons olive oil, 2 tablespoons balsamic vinegar, 1 clove minced garlic, 2 teaspoons sugar, $\frac{1}{4}$ teaspoon poppy seeds, and black pepper to taste. Pour dressing over salad and toss.

Sparkling Strawberry Punch: Blend 2 pounds strawberries in a food processor or blender until completely smooth. Mix in a serving bowl with 4 cups ginger ale, 4 cups sparkling mineral water, and 1 cup orange juice. Serves eight.

Strawberry Pizza: Make one recipe of Bisquick biscuit dough and roll it out $\frac{1}{8}$ inch thick. Cut into circles. Bake at 450 degrees on an ungreased pan for six minutes. Blend 8 ounces cream cheese with the grated rind of one orange and $\frac{1}{3}$ cup confectioners' sugar. Cut 1 pint of strawberries into slices. Top biscuits with cream cheese mixture and bake in a 425-degree oven for 3 minutes. Remove from oven, top with strawberries, sift a little confectioners' sugar over each, and serve warm. Makes 16 individual pizzas.

Lincoln listened carefully as Douglas defended the Supreme Court's decision. Lincoln believed in the rule of law, but he also believed the Court had made the wrong ruling in this case. "The Dred Scott decision is erroneous," he declared, based on "assumed historical facts which were not really true." He hoped that the Court would overrule its Dred Scott decision.

Lincoln's views were applauded by the members of the new Republican Party. When they met to choose a candidate for the upcoming Senate election, there was only one man, they agreed, who could stand against Douglas: "Illinois is for Abraham Lincoln!" Lincoln accepted their nomination with a thundering speech. In it, he warned against the spread of slavery, predicting a time when it could be

Dred Scott

"OYEZ! OYEZ! OYEZ!"

Our federal justice system has district courts, circuit courts, and one court that reigns supreme. If your case is tried in a lower court and you feel justice has not been served, you have the right to appeal—that is, to ask a higher court to hear your case. The Supreme Court, made up of nine justices, is the last place to go in the American judicial system.

When the justices meet to try cases, they all shake hands. "Oyez! Oyez! Oyez! The Court is now sitting!" cries the court marshal. ("Oyez," which means "Hear ye," is a word from medieval times.) For each case, the justices read the documents, give the opposing sides 30 minutes each to argue their cases, then take a vote (the majority vote wins). A Supreme Court decision can only be changed by another Supreme Court decision or by amending the Constitution.

Want to get a job on the Supreme Court? You have to be appointed by the president and get approval from the Senate. Be prepared to wear a uniform (a long black robe) every day. You'll serve for life in one of the most important jobs in the United States.

"lawful in all the states, old as well as new—North as well as South."

The arguments over slavery had gone on for years, Lincoln explained, and had only grown worse with time. "In my opinion," he said, "it will not cease, until a crisis shall have been reached and passed." He told his audience, "a house divided against itself cannot stand. I believe this government cannot endure, permanently half slave and half free. I do not expect the Union to be dissolved—I do not expect the house to fall—but I do expect it will cease to be divided. It will become all one thing or all the other."

The race for the Senate was on. When told his opponent was Abraham Lincoln, Douglas said, "I shall have my hands full. He is as honest as he is shrewd." The contest began in Chicago, where Douglas spoke from his hotel balcony. Below, the faces of the eager crowd were lit by torchlight. He pronounced Lincoln's "house divided" speech a call for war. Lincoln spoke from the same balcony the following night. The entire street was crowded with people; others leaned out the windows of nearby buildings. Lincoln got a laugh from the crowd by pretending alarm at the thought of himself, "poor, kind, and amiable," under fire from opponent Douglas. He denied that his speech was a call for war and said he did not mean to interfere with slavery where it already existed. He held on to his hope that by confining slavery to the existing states it would eventually fade away.

Lincoln challenged Douglas to a series of official debates. The candidates agreed to seven public debates to be held in different towns over two months. In addition to these debates, Lincoln and Douglas each made dozens of speeches in small and large towns across Illinois, traveling thousands of miles by train, boat, and carriage. The political battle in Illinois riveted the nation. The speeches made by Lincoln and Douglas were printed in newspapers and read by citizens across the country.

Douglas and his wife traveled from town to town in style, their private train car decorated with banners. As his train pulled into town, a brass cannon, loaded on a flatcar, announced Stephen A. Douglas's arrival with a thunderous roar. Lincoln left Mary at home and crisscrossed Illinois's prairies in a passenger car, preferring to sit with the regular travelers.

"The Great Debate at Ottawa," as one newspaper described it, brought 10,000 people to the small Illinois town to witness the Lincoln and Douglas rivalry. They came, on horseback and in carriages, from nearby farms. Special trains brought carloads of observers from more distant towns. Lincoln was escorted to Ottawa's town square by brass bands and a military company. Douglas disembarked from his train car a few miles outside of town and entered at the head of a grand procession with flags and banners flying.

The candidates agreed to take turns going first; in Ottawa, Douglas launched the debates. His booming voice carried over the crowd. He paced and gestured while he spoke. Douglas was an aggressive debater, once described

Lincoln-Douglas Debate ❖ Jeff Herbert

as being like a bomb that "bursts and sends red-hot nails in every direction." He came out hard to put Lincoln on the defense. "Hit him again!" voices cried from the crowd.

Lincoln stood up to reply. Tall and angular, dressed in black, his voice steady and high-pitched, he was a complete contrast to his opponent. According to his law partner Herndon, Lincoln "stood square on his feet" when speaking, "both of his legs straight up and down, toe even with toe." He did not gesture like Douglas, but at first held his hands behind his back, then clasped them in front, only occasionally raising the forefinger of his long right hand to make a point.

The candidates argued about popular sovereignty and the Kansas-Nebraska Act, the Dred Scott decision, and Negro equality. Douglas claimed that the framers "made this government divided into free states and slave states, and left each state perfectly free to do as it pleased on the subject of slavery. Why can it not exist on the same principles on which our fathers made it?" No, answered Lincoln, the government was "instituted to secure the blessings of freedom." He said that when Douglas "invites any people willing to have slavery, to establish it, he is blowing out the moral lights around us."

At that time, racial prejudice was widespread. Even Lincoln, who hated slavery, felt

HOLD A DEBATE

"**R**ESOLVED THAT CATS ARE BETTER THAN DOGS." You might have strong feelings one way or another about that statement, but a good debater could convince an audience either way. A good debater has excellent research skills, verbal skills that can dazzle an audience, and the ability to think quickly.

WHAT YOU NEED

- 2 to 6 debaters
- 3-by-5-inch index cards
- Pens
- Notebooks
- Chairperson
- Audience
- Tables
- Chairs
- Glasses of water
- Nametags
- Watch

Choose a topic for your debate and frame it as a resolution (a formal statement of opinion). You might use topics from Lincoln's era, such as:

Resolved: Slavery should be decided by the people of each state.

Resolved: A slave who has once lived in a free state should be considered free.

Resolved: Slavery is morally wrong.

Divide debaters into two teams. The Affirmative Team will argue that the statement is true. The Negative Team will argue against it. In the Lincoln-Douglas Debates, the first debater spoke for an hour, the second for an hour and a half, and then the first speaker had a half-hour to close. If you have only two debaters, you might choose this order (but limit your speeches to minutes). For two three-member teams, you might divide the debate order into four parts:

1. The Affirmative Team leader introduces the team's point of view and lists points supporting it. The Negative Team leader introduces their opposing point of view. (Two and a half minutes each.)

2. A second Affirmative Team member expands on the points supporting the team's point of view. A second Negative Team member does the same. (Five minutes each.)

3. A third Affirmative Team member tries to prove wrong all the arguments offered by the opposing team. A third Negative Team member does the same. (Five minutes each.)

4. The Affirmative Team leader summarizes their argument. The Negative Team leader gives their summary. No new arguments are allowed. (Two and a half minutes each.)

Decide on duties, debating order, and length of debate. Use the library and the Internet to obtain facts supporting your point of view. Research the opposing team's point of view so you are ready to argue them. Note quotes, facts, and their sources in case you are questioned.

Write and memorize your opening speech. Use index cards to organize facts that will help you defend your arguments or challenge your opponents'. Bring pens and notebooks to the debate to take notes during opposing arguments.

The chairperson should set up a table for each team with chairs, glasses of water, and nametags. When the audience is seated, the chairperson introduces the debaters, announces the resolution, and calls on the Affirmative Team leader to speak. Use a watch to note the time, and let the speaker know when his or her time is up. Call on and keep time for each debater.

Debaters, remember to stand up straight and make eye contact with audience members. Say, "Honored Chairperson, ladies and gentlemen." Speak clearly and be precise. Make logical arguments that are supported by the research you have done. Listen carefully when opponents speak so you can refute their arguments.

Finally, the chairperson should thank the teams and ask the audience to help declare the winner with a show of hands. Everyone should applaud both teams for their efforts.

blacks and whites could probably not live together as equals. That notion may not be just or sound, he said, but it was common and could not safely be ignored. Lincoln, like many others, thought colonization was a possibility for freed blacks. "My first impulse would be to free all the slaves," he said in this debate, "and send them to Liberia—to their own native land." But he acknowledged that this wasn't a very practical or even likely solution.

Douglas played on the audience's racism by calling Lincoln a "Black Republican." "I ask you," he cried, "are you in favor of conferring upon the negro the rights and privileges of citizenship?" What would happen, he asked the crowds, if freed slaves flooded into their state and tried to work and live side by side with whites? Lincoln replied that the Negro is entitled to all the rights listed in the Declaration of Independence, and, "in the right to eat the bread, without leave of anybody else, which his own hand earns, *he is my equal and the equal of Judge Douglas, and the equal of every living man.*"

In Ottawa, the debate ended with cheering crowds carrying the candidates home on their shoulders. Then it was on to Freeport, where an even bigger crowd gathered. In Jonesboro the crowds were small and no one cheered. In Charleston, the streets were filled, shoulder to shoulder, with people. In Galesburg, the local newspaper said Lincoln got in "a good hit" and "star-spangled banners were numberless." A Quincy paper said he supported Negro equality and denounced him for it. In Alton, Lincoln's wife, Mary, and their son Robert came to see the debate. Douglas declared his view that the Union could go on with "each state having the right to prohibit, abolish, or sustain slavery." Slavery was a cancer, Lin-

Lincoln, just before delivering his speech at the Cooper Institute ❖ Library of Congress

"He who would be no slave, must consent to have no slave. Those who deny freedom to others, deserve it not for themselves."

—Abraham Lincoln

coln replied. "It is the only thing that has ever threatened the existence of this Union." The Alton paper, in its article about this last debate, called on its readers to listen to both sides and "judge them by their merits."

Lincoln went home and waited for Election Day. In spite of his great efforts, he lost the Senate seat to Douglas. He was devastated. He told his friends, "I feel like the boy who stumped his toe. I am too big to cry and too badly hurt to laugh." Still, he was glad to have made the attempts, even though "I now sink out of view, and shall be forgotten."

Lincoln was not forgotten. The debates with Douglas brought him national fame—and invitations to speak. He took trains to Ohio, Wisconsin, and Kansas, delivering speeches that made people sit up and think about the tall prairie lawyer. Some began to believe he could become president.

Invited to speak in New York City, Lincoln bought a new suit and took a train to the East. At first, the refined New York audience was taken aback by the awkward-looking country lawyer and his midwestern twang. "Thank you, Mr. Cheermun," Lincoln began. But his speech at the Cooper Institute was so powerful that the audience forgot about his quaint accent and unfashionable clothes. As he spoke, they listened so intently that the only sound was the sizzle of gas lamps. He urged

JOHN BROWN AND HARPERS FERRY

"**T**alk! Talk! Talk!" cried John Brown, "That will never free the slaves! Action is needed!" He plotted to ignite a slave uprising in Harpers Ferry, Virginia. With a small group of men, including his sons, Brown took over a federal arsenal in that town, intending to distribute its weapons to slaves who would flock to his side. The uprising never occurred. Brown was captured by marines under the command of Lieutenant Colonel Robert E. Lee, found guilty of treason by the state of Virginia, and hanged.

John Brown's raid caused panic in the Southern states, where people feared slave uprisings. They blamed Northern abolitionists and the Republican Party for Brown's attack. In the North, many thought Brown's actions were wrong but his motives noble. There, church bells tolled at his death. The badly divided country split even further. When Congress next met after Brown's hanging, most of the congressmen came to Washington armed with guns.

John Brown

them, "Let us not be slandered from our duty by false accusations against us, nor frightened from it by menaces of destruction to the government nor of dungeons to ourselves. *Let us have faith that right makes might, and in that faith, let us, to the end, dare to do our duty as*

we understand it!" The audience jumped to its feet and cheered wildly.

Newspapers printed Lincoln's Cooper Institute speech. When he left New York to visit his son Robert (then attending private school on the East Coast), Lincoln was called on to give speeches everywhere he went. More and more, people spoke of him as a likely candidate for the presidency. On his return home after the trip, when asked about the possibility, Lincoln replied, "I will be entirely frank. The taste *is* in my mouth a little."

Months later, the Republican Party met in Chicago to choose a presidential candidate. Lincoln did not attend the convention but stayed home in Springfield while supporters put his name forward. He played handball in a vacant lot, wandered to his office, then headed to the newspaper office to hear the latest news from Chicago. There, he was handed a telegram and looked at it for a long time. "Well," he said, "we've got it." Lincoln had been nominated for the presidency. Nominated for the vice-presidency was Hannibal Hamlin, a New Englander who strongly opposed slavery. Lincoln walked back to the vacant lot, where his friends were still playing handball. "Shake my hand while you can!" he joked, then said he'd better go. "There is a little woman at our house who is probably more interested in this dispatch than I am." The word of his nomina-

tion spread quickly. As Lincoln walked home, church bells rang and cannons boomed in celebration.

Northern and Southern Democrats had not been able to agree on issues or their candidate. Their party split in two. The South nominated John C. Breckinridge; Northern Democrats nominated Lincoln's rival Stephen A. Douglas. The Constitutional Union Party entered the contest too, with nominee John Bell of Tennessee.

In those days it was not considered proper for a presidential candidate to promote himself (though Douglas traveled and campaigned until he lost his voice). While Lincoln stayed home in Springfield, friends and supporters worked on his behalf. Across the North, Republican "Wide-Awake Clubs" held rallies and parades to stir up support for Lincoln. The Wide-Awakes (who got their name because they marched at night by torchlight) wore black caps and capes. They carried rails to represent their candidate—"Abraham Lincoln, The Rail Splitter, For President in 1860!"

In the South, newspapers pronounced Lincoln a "blood-thirsty tyrant" and a "scoundrelly" abolitionist. Threats of secession increased. "The South will never submit to such humiliation and degradation as the inauguration of Abraham Lincoln!" claimed one newspaper.

LINCOLN CELEBRATED his New York trip by visiting daguerreotype artist Mathew Brady's studio. One of the earliest form of photography, the daguerreotype captured images on silver-coated copper plates. Sitters held completely still for the long minutes it took to expose the plates, and were told not to smile because it was too hard to hold a smile for that length of time.

Because they were so precious, daguerreotypes were framed in brass and enclosed in small leather cases. Velvet material protected the image. Elaborate designs decorated the case.

Adult supervision required

WHAT YOU NEED

- Thick cardboard (from a heavy box), 4½ by 6 inches
- Pencil
- Scissors
- White glue
- Piece of red velvet, 3 by 4½ inches
- Sheet of soft copper (.005 thick, 36 gauge), 3 by 4½ inches, or gold ribbon, 15 inches long by ½ inch wide
- Paper clip
- 1 hook and eye (can purchase at fabric store)
- Small piece of thin cardboard
- Dark brown marker
- Needle and thread

- Standard camera with black-and-white film, or digital camera and access to computer and printer
- Pink marker

The thick piece of cardboard will be the case for your daguerreotype. Fold it in half, like a book.

With the pencil, draw flowers, hearts, and curlicues on the thin piece of cardboard. Cut them out and glue them on the front of the case. Use the dark brown marker to color the front and back of the case (including the cutouts) so it looks like leather.

Open the case and glue the red velvet to the left-hand side. *If you are using a copper sheet:* carefully fold each edge of the copper sheet under and glue that side of the sheet to the right-hand side of the case; pull apart the paper clip and use the pointy edge to carve ornate designs around the edges of the copper sheet. *If you are using gold ribbon:* cut the ribbon and glue it around the edges of the right-hand side of the case.

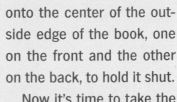

Sew the hook and eye onto the center of the outside edge of the book, one on the front and the other on the back, to hold it shut.

Now it's time to take the photograph. Have your subject dress up (maybe in 19th-century style!). He or she should pose seated and looking straight at the camera, or standing, perhaps with a hand resting on a table or book. Remember—no smiling! Use a digital camera or a camera loaded with black-and-white film. If using regular film, have it developed.

You can make a black-and-white photograph look old by scanning it and using photo-editing software to change its colors to a sepia tone. If you are using a digital camera, download your photograph and do the same. Print the photograph. Daguerreotype artists sometimes "colorized" their images with powdered pigment. Lightly touch up your subject's cheeks with the pink marker. Glue the photograph on top of the copper sheet or in the middle of the ribbon inside the case.

While the months passed and the campaign progressed, Lincoln's office was swamped by reporters, photographers, well-wishers, and people who hoped for favors if he became president. He moved into an office in the state capitol building and hired a young man, John Nicolay, as his secretary. Nicolay kept visitors at bay and helped Lincoln with his increasingly large amount of correspondence.

Among the many letters Lincoln received was one from 11-year-old Grace Bedell of Westfield, New York. Grace had seen a picture of Lincoln and wrote to him suggesting that he grow a beard. "All the ladies like whiskers," she said, "and they would tease their husbands to vote for you." Lincoln kindly replied to her letter, and asked her if she didn't think people might find it silly. But he grew a beard anyway.

On Election Day, Lincoln stretched out on a couch in the Springfield telegraph office to wait for news. Congratulatory telegrams ar-

A PRESIDENTIAL BEARD

ABRAHAM LINCOLN was the first president to wear a beard. Why wait until you're president? Make one out of felt today.

Adult supervision required

WHAT YOU NEED

- Scissors
- Black felt, 2 inches wide and 12 inches long
- Ruler
- 3 pins
- Needle and black thread
- Two rubber bands
- Stapler

Cut the felt so that it resembles the shape of a banana, as shown. The straight part in the middle, before it turns up at the ends, should be 6 inches long.

Gather the material in the very center to make a fold ¼ inch wide at the bottom and tapering to a point. Pin it. Measure 1½ inches to the left and right of the middle fold and make two more identical folds. Pin them. Use needle and thread to sew the folds from base to point. These folds will help fit the beard around your chin.

Hold the beard up to your face. The ends should come close to your ears. Cut any extra material from the ends.

Staple the rubber bands 1 inch below each end. To put on the beard, fit a rubber band around each ear.

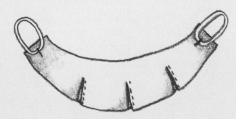

Rally in New York

rived from state after state until it finally became clear that Lincoln had won. When the news got out, Springfield's men threw their hats in the air and cheered. People locked arms and paraded, singing, down the streets.

Lincoln pushed his way through crowds of smiling friends who cheered and called him "Mr. President!" With the last telegram in his pocket, he walked home. "Mary," he cried, "we are elected!"

"A TASK BEFORE ME"

As Abraham Lincoln's train chugged its way to Washington, curious crowds gathered at railroad depots to get a look at the president-elect. In some towns, he gave a short speech. In others, he simply appeared on the rear platform of his train car so that, he joked, people could observe "my very interesting" appearance. "I came so that I may see you and you may see me," he told them, "and in the arrangement I have the best of the bargain!"

Lincoln deliberately avoided saying much about what was on everyone's mind—the secession crisis. In the month after Lincoln's election, South Carolina had declared that the union between it and the United States of America "is hereby dissolved." South Carolinians went wild with excitement, celebrating their secession with parades and fireworks displays. While Lincoln packed his trunks, the people of Mississippi,

Florida, Alabama, Georgia, Louisiana, and Texas cut their ties to the Union. As his train pushed east, the seceded states joined together as the Confederate States of America, and named their own president, Jefferson Davis. The constitution of the new Confederacy would read very much like the Constitution of the United States, except for the declaration that slavery would be "recognized and protected."

Leaving Springfield had not been easy for Lincoln. There had been much to attend to—including the swarms of job-seekers, reporters, old friends, and the simply curious who

[LEFT] *"Lincoln Compares Heights"* ❖ Indiana Historical Society [BELOW] *Jefferson Finis Davis*

hounded the president-elect. They peered over Lincoln's fence as he chopped wood and milked his cow, and lined up at his office to ask for favors. Lincoln's hand ached from constant congratulatory handshakes. His secretary, John Nicolay, had to hire his own assistant, John Hay, to help with the mountains of correspondence.

Lincoln welcomed his visitors and listened patiently to their concerns, then locked himself in his office to work on his inaugural speech. He stayed up nights making lists of people who could serve in his cabinet. He responded to worried letters that begged him to do something about the seceding Southern states. "We must compromise!" people said anxiously, "and not let the Union dissolve!" Lincoln disagreed. "Let there be no compromise on the question of extending slavery," he wrote. "Stand firm. The tug has to come, and better now, than anytime hereafter." Besides, he didn't really believe that secession would last. "The people of the South have too much sense to attempt the ruin of the government," he said.

Between one presidency and the next, as the threats to secede became a reality, the country held its breath. What would Lincoln do? In the meantime, outgoing president Buchanan was at a loss. He gave a speech saying both that the Southerners had no right to secede

JEFFERSON DAVIS VS. ABRAHAM LINCOLN

While Lincoln took his inaugural train trip across the country, Jefferson Finis Davis traveled by boat and train from his Mississippi plantation to Montgomery, Alabama. Davis had been asked to lead the new Confederate States of America.

Jefferson Davis was born in a Kentucky log cabin, only miles and months apart from Abraham Lincoln. But he was a college and West Point graduate while Lincoln had only one year of schooling. They both served in the Black Hawk War, but Davis fought in the Mexican War while Lincoln objected to it. Davis was a prominent Washington insider, a former senator and secretary of war. Lincoln had served one modest term in Congress. Davis was haughty, quick-tempered, and serious. Lincoln was good-natured, humorous, and, as a friend put it, "a very poor hater."

In towns across the North, Lincoln was besieged by crowds who pushed and jostled to get a glimpse of the president-elect. Some greeted him with cheers; others watched silently, wondering what kind of man would be leading their country. Davis and his vice president, Alexander Stephens—a friend of Lincoln's from his days in Congress—rode into Montgomery in a carriage drawn by six white horses. Bands played military songs, ladies threw bouquets, and thousands of Southerners cheered the man with the deep-set eyes who would be their president.

and that the government had no right to stop them. Privately, he told his friends he thought he would be the last president of the United States.

THE PRESIDENT'S CABINET

Like all presidents since George Washington, Lincoln chose a cabinet—not a piece of furniture, but a group of advisers who would lead important departments and help him make decisions. If you were president, whom would you put in charge of the Defense or Treasury departments? Trusted best friends or experts you don't know? Lincoln did not personally know the men he chose to advise him. His cabinet of seven strong-willed men included several who had been his rivals for the presidential nomination.

At the start, Secretary of State William Seward thought he would be able to boss Lincoln around, but Lincoln made it clear that *he* was president. Seward, who told jokes and liked to belch loudly, became one of Lincoln's best friends. Secretary of War Simon Cameron served only nine months, then resigned because of scandals. Opinionated Edwin M. Stanton, who had once called Lincoln

William H. Seward

Gideon Welles

"a long-armed ape," took Cameron's place and came to revere the president. Stanton was so energetic that Lincoln jokingly suggested someone put bricks in his pockets to keep him down. Secretary of the Treasury Salmon P. Chase had his eye on the presidency (friends claimed he looked in the mirror every day and said, "Good morning, Mr. President!") and tried to gain it in 1864. Lincoln named him U.S. chief justice later that year. Lincoln called Gideon Welles, his secretary of the navy, "Father Neptune," because of his long, white beard.

These and Lincoln's other advisers all had different ideas about how to run the country. They quarreled with each other. Early on, more than one thought, "Lincoln doesn't know what he's doing. I should be president!" Lincoln listened to their counsel and kept an open mind, then made up his own about what to do. He learned when to trust their strong opinions and when to trust his own.

While many people still thought a compromise would bring the seceded states back to the fold, others said, "Let them go." If the country can only survive with slavery, said abolitionist William Lloyd Garrison, let the country dissolve. "It's anarchy!" exclaimed others; if this minority leaves because they didn't get their way, why, that's the end of all government! The South must be forced to remain in the Union, and Lincoln must force them, even if blood must be shed.

In the South, many did not think it would come to war. People told each other that any blood spilled over secession could be wiped up with a handkerchief.

Before leaving for Washington, Mary took a train trip to New York City to purchase the latest dresses, gloves, and shoes. Lincoln missed his wife and walked to the train station night after night, hoping for her return. He went by train and buggy to see his elderly stepmother and visit his father's grave. Sarah Lincoln cried at the thought of her stepson's future. She had not wanted him to run for the presidency, fearing that something bad would happen to him. Lincoln said good-bye to the woman who had been such a "good and kind mother" to him, promising her they would see each other again.

Back in Springfield, he stopped at his law office one last time and told his partner to leave

Saying good-bye to Springfield (a reenactment) ❧ Lincoln Home National Historic Site

the "Lincoln & Herndon" sign over the door. "Billy," he said, "if I live, I'm coming back some time, and then we'll go right on practicing law as if nothing had ever happened."

On the morning he left Springfield, Lincoln shook hands with his neighbors and walked to the train depot. It was rainy and gloomy, and he was sad to leave. He stood on the back of his train car as friends gathered to say farewell. "To this place and the kindness of these people I owe everything," he said. "I now leave,

not knowing when, or whether ever, I may return, with a task before me greater than that which rested upon Washington." He asked for their help and their prayers, and then his train pulled away.

Assistants Nicolay and Hay went to Washington with the Lincolns. A friend, Ward Lamon, came along as bodyguard—and brought his banjo, too. To the delight of the Lincoln children, family friend Elmer Ellsworth joined the party. This lively young man

NORTH AND SOUTH

The new **Confederacy** and the country it had seceded from were two very different places. Of the 30 million people who lived in the United States in 1860, 21 million lived in the North. Northern cities and industries attracted new immigrants. The North had more factories, more railroads, bridges, and roads. Of the 9 million people who lived in the Confederacy, 4 million were slaves. The South was "the land of cotton," with large plantations, small farms, and few factories.

Still, Jefferson Davis said that "the South is determined to maintain her position, and make all who oppose her smell southern powder and feel southern steel." In the rural South, men knew how to handle guns and horses. Many Southerners had attended military school and had served in the Mexican War. If it came to war, Southerners felt ready to defend their "sacred duty to rebel."

worked in Lincoln's law office. Lincoln and Mary were very fond of him, and thought of him almost as another son.

The trip was eventful. In small communities, people lined up along the tracks and cheered. In bigger towns, Lincoln was honored with receptions, music, and parades. In one town, a cannon salute shattered the windows of their train car. Robert Lincoln, nicknamed by the press "the Prince of Rails," made friends with the engineer and even got to drive the locomotive. He had so much fun he forgot that he was responsible for the satchel that held his father's inaugural speech. Everyone panicked when it disappeared, but Lincoln found it buried beneath a pile of luggage. Tad and Willie played pranks on people who were eager to get a glimpse of the president-elect. "Want to see old Abe?" they'd ask, then point to someone else.

Some were surprised when they saw Lincoln for the first time. "We were seriously disappointed in the physique of the President elect," wrote a reporter. Lincoln bowed awkwardly and wore black gloves instead of proper white ones. People did not know what to make of this western giant, who laughed at his own jokes and said "git" for "get" and "thar" for "there." But his sincerity and good nature won them over.

In Westfield, New York, Lincoln asked if Grace Bedell was in the crowd. The girl who had suggested he grow a beard was pushed to the front and got a kiss from Abraham Lincoln. In Buffalo, he played an undignified game of leapfrog with his two younger sons and the son of the hotelkeeper. "He didn't act like a president!" said the boy.

After Lincoln made a hurried and secretive entry into Washington, newspapers said

the same thing—but they did not mean it as a compliment. Even back in Springfield, Lincoln had received death threats. When he got to Philadelphia he was warned that assassins planned to kill him as his train went through Baltimore, Maryland. "You will never pass through that city alive," detectives told him. They urged him to skip his last speeches and change to another train so he could enter Washington safely.

Lincoln insisted on giving his promised talks. At Philadelphia's Independence Hall he praised the Declaration of Independence and its promise of liberty. "If this country cannot be saved without giving up that principle," he said and then paused. "I was about to say I would rather be assassinated on this spot than to surrender it." After his next talk, Lincoln threw his coat over his shoulders and disguised himself by exchanging his stovepipe hat for a soft felt one. As he boarded a special train, detectives cut telegraph wires so no word could get out that Lincoln had left town.

In the dark of night, Lincoln was hurried on to another train car. Bodyguard Ward Lamon kept his hands on his pistols as the car rocked through the night and the empty streets of Baltimore. Lincoln arrived safely in Washington at dawn; his family came on a later train. Newspaper reporters mocked Lincoln for his secretive entry into Washington. Political

YOU SEE Abraham Lincoln every day! Make a game of it.

WHAT YOU NEED

☒ Pencil ☒ Friends
☒ Paper

Hold a contest with your friends—see how many times in a week you can spot Abraham Lincoln's name or image. You might be surprised how often he appears. A 50-foot statue of Lincoln peers over a summit in Wyoming; a dignified statue greets Londoners on their daily commute.

He shows up in poems, plays, books, and movies. Lincoln even appeared on an episode of *Star Trek*! Look for statues, ads, and street signs. Keep a list and compare notes. Make a stovepipe hat (see page 40) for the winner.

Need some clues? Here are some places to spot Old Abe (count each only once):

☒ On a coin and a bill   ☒ Toys
☒ A city in Nebraska   ☒ A U.S. highway
☒ A financial company   ☒ In movies
☒ Carved into a   ☒ A car
   mountain

THROUGHOUT LINCOLN'S PRESIDENCY, everyone had an opinion about how he was running the country. Some expressed their opinions in political cartoons, which lampoon people and comment on current events with drawings and captions that use caricature and symbolism. Now, sharpen your pencils and sharpen your wit—political cartooning is harder than it looks!

WHAT YOU NEED
- Recent newspapers and news magazines
- Pencils
- Eraser
- Notebook
- Drawing paper
- Fine-tipped markers

Immerse yourself in the news for a month. Read newspapers and news magazines and study current events. Keep notes in your notebook. Develop your own opinions about the issues, then pick a topic for your cartoon and decide on your point of view. (As a political cartoonist, you can express negative or positive opinions.)

Clip and collect political cartoons and spend some time analyzing their different elements. Cartoonists use symbols (like Uncle Sam for the U.S.). The cartoon on the right shows symbols that people in 1860 clearly understood. Abraham Lincoln and Stephen A. Douglas run toward their goal, Washington (a visual pun on the phrase "presidential race"). The rail fence symbolizes Lincoln's past as a rail-splitter. Douglas is hampered by the burden he carries—a jug stamped "M.C." (for Missouri Compromise). The black man represents slavery.

Cartoonists also use caricature. The 1860 cartoon exaggerated Lincoln's long legs and Douglas's small size as a way of showing that Lincoln had an advantage in the political race.

Think of symbols that represent a dilemma or situation your subject faces. What kind of setting will you put your subject in? A boxing ring? A schoolroom? How would caricature help you make your point? Write drafts of ideas and make rough sketches in your notebook. Keep your audience in mind. Your visual references should be immediately clear to them. Play with references to history or images from popular culture. Try using animal images (is your subject acting like a chicken? a snake in the grass?).

Experiment with drawing caricatures of your subjects. By exaggerating features, you can poke fun, show admiration, or emphasize personality traits. For example, a huge forehead might imply that the person is very brainy; an overly muscular character might be seen as a bully. You might be able to play on words or names, too. For example, with a name like Salmon Chase, Lincoln's secretary of the treasury could have been drawn as a fish.

You can use dialogue between characters to further make your point. Draw bubbles or squares to contain the words that characters are thinking or saying, or write a caption that perfectly expresses your views.

Once you are satisfied with your rough draft, draw your cartoon in pencil. Now you are ready to "ink it," or go over the penciled drawing with markers. Show your cartoon masterpiece to friends. You might even submit it to your local newspaper for its editorial page.

Lincoln and Douglas in a presidential footrace
Library of Congress

cartoons showed him arriving in Washington, peeking out of a railroad boxcar, wearing a Scottish tam.

John Hay was appalled. Washington smelled "like 20,000 drowned cats!" he said. Its 60,000 residents lived in one- and two-story wood or brick homes. Visitors stayed at boarding houses or the famous Willard's Hotel. Their carriages got stuck in deep winter mud; in summer, horses kicked up dust that covered everything. Summer also brought mosquitoes and terrible heat. Geese, chickens, pigs, and cows roamed the streets. Flies buzzed around the meat and fruit at outdoor markets. Water, obtained from wells or springs, was sometimes tainted.

With its large vacant lots and the half-finished Washington Monument, the city felt incomplete. The domeless Capitol Building was covered with scaffolding. Its construction had come to a halt, but Lincoln insisted that work on the building resume, as a sign that the Union would go on.

All the talk in Washington was of secession. Everyone wondered what the new president would do. Other Southern states were threatening to follow the seven that had already left the Union. The seceded states had begun to take over federal mints, arsenals, and forts within their borders, and to seize their supplies and weapons. They demanded that the

"Balloon View of Washington, D.C."
Library of Congress

federal troops still holding forts surrender and leave. Soon, the only Southern forts still flying a United States flag were in Florida and one, Fort Sumter, in the harbor of Charleston, South Carolina. The federal soldiers holding Fort Sumter tightened their belts. Their food and supplies were running low. In the meantime, visitors at Lincoln's hotel stood in line to meet him. Many begged him to avoid a crisis— maybe even war—by evacuating Fort Sumter.

On Inauguration Day, Washington looked as if a war had already begun. Rumors had spread of assassination threats and plots to kidnap the president during his inaugural. Winfield Scott, the nation's elderly, portly, and commanding general in chief, placed sharpshooters on rooftops and ordered cavalry troops to flank Lincoln's carriage. Howitzers pointed down the city's streets. Detectives mingled with the crowds, and General Scott himself stood guard on Capitol Hill.

When Lincoln stepped out onto the inaugural platform, the crowd peered curiously at the tall man in the black suit. He removed his stovepipe hat and looked around, unsure where to place it. Senator Stephen Douglas stepped forward from a line of dignitaries and kindly offered to hold the hat of his one-time rival. Lincoln put on his spectacles and read his inaugural address. His high voice carried over the crowd.

It was not lawful, Lincoln told them, for states to withdraw from the United States. He considered the Union to be unbroken. He

United States Capitol Building under construction ❖ Library of Congress

made it clear that the federal government intended to keep and hold all of its forts. He assured Southerners that he intended to support the existing laws protecting slavery, and he urged the people of the South to think calmly about their next actions. "In *your* hands, my dissatisfied fellow countrymen, and not in *mine* is the momentous issue of civil war. The government will not assail you. *You* can have no conflict, without being yourselves the aggressors. *You* have no oath registered in Heaven to destroy the government, while I shall have the most solemn one to 'preserve, protect, and defend' it."

Lincoln was reluctant to end his speech. "We are not enemies, but friends," he said. "We must not be enemies. Though passion may have strained, it must not break our bonds of affection. The mystic chords of memory, stretching from every battle-field, and patriot grave, to every living heart and hearthstone, all over this broad land, will yet swell the chorus of the Union, when again touched, as surely they will be, by the better angels of our nature." His speech ended, Lincoln was sworn in as the 16th president of the United States.

Years before, during the Black Hawk War, Lincoln had been sworn in to the Illinois militia by Lieutenant Robert Anderson. The day after his inauguration, President Lincoln sat at his desk and read a report from Anderson, now a major in command of Fort Sumter. Major Anderson wrote that the fort was surrounded by Confederate guns and its supplies were dangerously low. Within six weeks, there would be no food left.

Lincoln had to do something. Should he send reinforcements? If he sent more troops, they would surely be attacked, possibly sparking a war. He could abandon the fort altogether, avoiding a confrontation. But that meant going back on his inaugural pledge to hold all federal properties in the South. Plus, abandoning Fort Sumter would tell the world that the United States government was resigned to losing not just its forts but the newly seceded states as well.

"Evacuate!" said most of Lincoln's cabinet advisers. "Reinforce!" screamed newspaper headlines. Lincoln didn't know what to do. For weeks, he agonized over the decision; his worries sent him to bed with migraine headaches. Finally, he made up his mind. He sent word to South Carolina's governor that he intended to send only food and supplies—no weapons or ammunition—to Fort Sumter. He ordered ships loaded with provisions to set sail.

Before the ships even arrived, Confederate president Jefferson Davis demanded Fort Sumter's surrender. When Major Anderson refused, the Confederates opened fire. More than 4,000 rounds bombarded the fort while

Lincoln's inauguration

A SOLEMN OATH

When he was sworn in to office, Lincoln (like all presidents) promised to "preserve, protect, and defend the Constitution." The Constitution defines the basic laws and functions of the United States government. It establishes how laws are created and how officials are elected. It outlines the roles of the president, Congress, and the Supreme Court. It outlines the rights of citizens. The Constitution can be amended (changed), but only if two-thirds of Congress and three-fourths of the states agree.

In Lincoln's time, the Constitution protected slavery in the states where it already existed. As president, he was bound by his oath to protect the rights of slaveholders.

Fort Sumter

Charleston's residents watched, cheering, from their rooftops. Two days later, Major Anderson surrendered and the Confederate flag was raised over Fort Sumter. War had begun.

The next day, Lincoln put out a proclamation for 75,000 90-day volunteers. Most soldiers in the regular United States Army, only 16,000 men strong, were serving on the western frontier. It would take some time to gather those forces and increase their numbers.

Across the North, people held rallies and parades, waved flags, and shouted for union. Though the governors of states bordering the Confederacy objected to the call for militia,

other states promised to send help. Lincoln's young friend Elmer Ellsworth went to New York City to recruit men he claimed were "soldiers ready made"—New York's firemen. While men in Northern towns and farm communities enlisted, drilled, and prepared for soldiering, four more states (Virginia, Arkansas, North Carolina, and Tennessee) seceded from the Union. The Confederate government, which already had 60,000 troops ready, seized weapons from the federal arsenal at Harpers Ferry and prepared to make its capital in Richmond, Virginia.

Lincoln and other Washington residents felt surrounded. Only the Potomac River separated the nation's capital from Virginia. From his window, Lincoln peered through a telescope at the town of Alexandria, Virginia, and the Confederate flags waving from its highest buildings. Confederate troops drilled in Alexandria's streets. A force could easily sweep across the river and capture Washington!

Washington's residents worried, too, about the state of Maryland, which surrounded their city. Maryland had not seceded, but it was a slave state with many residents sympathetic to secession. As Northern militia companies gathered and made their way from various states to the city of Washington, they met with opposition as they traveled through Maryland. In Baltimore, crowds grew violent, shouting insults and throwing stones at railroad cars carrying militia companies. Many soldiers and civilians were killed.

Every day brought new rumors of menacing Confederate invasions and plans to kidnap President Lincoln. One senator recruited an emergency force to protect the White House; the armed men camped in the building's East Room. Another Washington official appeared at the door of the White House armed with three pistols and a bowie knife, vowing to pro-tect the president. An attack was imminent, warned General Scott. Lincoln drifted into the East Room and looked over the few guards camped there. Troubled, he looked out the windows of the White House, searching for signs of the promised militia. "Why don't they come?" he wondered aloud.

Finally, help arrived. Soon Washington's streets were crowded with marching militia companies and wagons loaded with supplies. The city was bursting with soldiers; some even

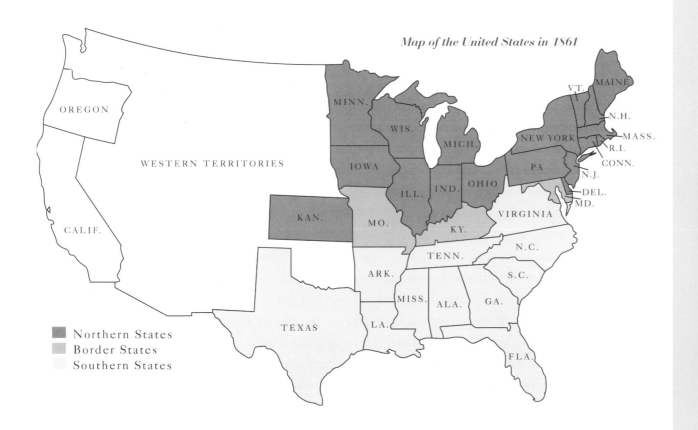

Map of the United States in 1861

- Northern States
- Border States
- Southern States

On the hills across the Potomac River from Washington stood Arlington Heights, the home of Robert E. Lee. Lee was one of the country's best soldiers. Lincoln hoped he would lead the Union army during this time of crisis and offered to make him general. Lee declined and joined the Confederacy, feeling he could not fight against his home state of Virginia. Other military officers followed him, leaving life-long careers in the Union army to fight for the South. Diplomats, government agents, and others joined them, packing their bags and returning to homes in the South.

Robert E. Lee ❦ National Archives

Soldiers camping in the East Room of the White House ❖ Library of Congress

and up its stairs to remove a Confederate flag flying from the roof. As he clattered back down the stairs, the innkeeper shot and killed him. Lincoln was devastated by the loss.

There was barely time to grieve. New regiments arrived daily, needing weapons and supplies. Petitioners arrived daily too, lining up by the hundreds outside the president's door. They each wanted something—a position in the government or a contract to sell goods; a son's exemption from duty or a generalship. Every day, Lincoln's secretaries, Nicolay and Hay, tried in vain to stem the flow of people. The White House was open to everyone in those days, and sometimes it seemed as if everyone was there. People sat on the staircases and crowded the halls.

Lincoln called his office his "shop." He arrived there early and, Hay said, would "go at" piles of documents like a man sawing wood. There were letters to answer, speeches to write, and decisions to make—many decisions, and each so pressing. How to keep the border states from seceding? How to convince Great Britain, a country sympathetic to the South, to stay out of the conflict? What to do with the fugitive slaves who ran to Union encampments? Who should lead the troops that were gathering in Washington?

General Winfield Scott had for long years been the country's greatest war hero, but he

made a makeshift camp in the House and Senate chambers. Ellsworth returned with his recruited New York firemen. Lincoln took heart. He called for more volunteers and for regulars for the U.S. Army and Navy.

In the meantime, General Scott sent soldiers across the bridges to Alexandria in the dark of night. The foray was a success and Alexandria was soon emptied of Confederate troops. But Lincoln paid a high personal price for this success. His young friend Ellsworth, leading his firemen through Alexandria, ran into a hotel was far too old to lead men in battle. He advised President Lincoln on war strategy. He suggested that the Union navy blockade Confederate coasts and the Mississippi River so no ships could leave or enter Southern ports. That way, the South would eventually run out of supplies. Scott's advice was good, but Lincoln needed a general to lead his troops. He chose Irvin McDowell, an honored veteran of the Mexican War.

While McDowell looked with concern at the new, untried troops, newspaper headlines urged, "Forward to Richmond!" Northerners were eager to strike the Southern capital and end the rebellion. But between Washington and Richmond stood the critical railroad junction of Manassas, near Bull Run Creek. Just 25 miles west of Washington, it was guarded by a large Rebel force. McDowell did not think his untrained troops were ready to make an attack. Our troops are green, Lincoln agreed, "but they are green, too. You are all green alike." He ordered McDowell to fight.

McDowell and his troops marched out of the city toward Bull Run Creek. By midafternoon, Lincoln could hear the distant rumble of big guns. Eager for news, he walked to General Scott's office, only to find the old man napping. Scott woke up and assured the president that the battle was going well. Restless, Lincoln went for a carriage ride. By the

CIVIL WAR OR WAR BETWEEN THE STATES?

A civil war is a war fought between citizens of the same nation. Lincoln never recognized the Confederacy as a separate country. He considered the secessionist actions to be a rebellion of individuals. In a July 4, 1861, message to Congress, Lincoln described the coming fight as the answer to whether or not a democracy can maintain itself "against its own domestic foes."

Northerners would fight a civil war, which they called the "War of the Rebellion." Northern men joined the army to save the Union. Government by the people was a new thing in the world. If this government failed, the hopes of all peoples for democracy would be shattered.

The Confederates thought differently. They were no longer the same nation—theirs would be a "War Between the States." Their battle cry was "states' rights!" The states had joined the Union voluntarily. Why couldn't they leave if they felt the government was not working on their behalf? Southerners felt they had a right to secede and choose a new government.

time he returned, the news had changed for the worse. The Union army had been put to flight, becoming entangled, in their hurried retreat, with the carriages of civilians who had gone to see the great battle. That night, Lincoln watched from his window as the defeated soldiers limped back into town, worn and wounded.

"WE MUST THINK ANEW, AND ACT ANEW."

"Charge!" the boys cried as they ran through the halls. Willie and Tad Lincoln thought living in the White House was a great adventure. They dressed in soldiers' uniforms. They built a fort on the roof to fire pretend cannons at pretend Rebels. They invaded a cabinet meeting as if it were a Confederate camp. They enlisted butlers and maids in their play, lining them up for drills.

Every day, Willie rode his much-loved pony, then let his little brother ride it too. Their goats, Nanny and Nanko, grazed on the White House grounds. Cats and rabbits and their dog, Jip, had the run of the house.

While their older brother Robert attended college, the two younger boys were tutored at home. Willie, the more thoughtful of the two, liked to read and write poetry. He memorized railroad timetables and took imaginary trips across the country. He collected newspaper articles to make a scrapbook of important events of the time. Tad was loving and kind but more playful than his brother, and full of mischief. He did not like to read or study.

He stole strawberries from the White House kitchen and demanded nickels from the people waiting to see his father. One time he even rode Nanko the goat into a formal reception! Both boys liked to join their father when he visited soldiers in the camps around Washington. They rode behind Lincoln as he reviewed the troops.

Whenever he could get away from the demands of his office, Lincoln played with the boys and their friends. He took his sons to see comedies at theaters, read to them, and told them stories. They pounced on him and wrestled him down. Sometimes they barged into his office, demanding attention. Once they came begging Lincoln to write a presidential pardon for Tad's doll, who was to be executed for sleeping at his post. "The Doll Jack is pardoned by order of the President," Lincoln wrote.

Mary Lincoln liked living in the White House too, but she found it shabby and in need of a makeover. The wallpaper was peeling and the floors scuffed. Some visitors even clipped pieces from the carpets and drapes to take home as souvenirs! Mary went to the finest shops in Philadelphia and New York to buy fancy French wallpaper, the most expensive furnishings and drapes, velvet carpet, and a new set of china. She also purchased gowns, shawls, and gloves, all in the latest fashions.

The Lincoln family at the White House
Library of Congress

LINCOLN WAS PROUD of Willie's scrapbook and showed it to friends. Pretend to be Willie Lincoln, living in the White House during the Civil War, and make a scrapbook of events and people of that time.

WHAT YOU NEED

- Internet access
- Printer
- Civil War magazines and newsletters
- Postcards from battlefields and Civil War sites
- Old maps
- Scissors
- Large, shallow box
- Selection of paper from craft store (choose colors, patterns, and textures that bring the Civil War era to mind—like blue and gray)
- Ruler
- Pens, colored pencils, or markers
- Scraps of cloth in different colors and textures
- White glue
- Glue stick
- Clear plastic sleeves for scrapbook pages
- Binder

Think about the subjects you would like to feature in your Civil War scrapbook. Each page will tell a story. Perhaps you would like to have a page dedicated to Abraham Lincoln and a page showing events that led up to the Civil War. Other topics include fashions and daily life of the 1860s, famous people of the era, or important battles. How about pages for Civil War artists or a particular soldier?

Pick your themes and collect related items and articles. You can find magazines dedicated to the Civil War in most bookstores. Look for inexpensive picture books, too. Contact friends and relatives around the country and ask them to mail postcards of Civil War battlefields and sites. Conduct Internet research and print the best items you find. You might discover Civil War drawings and photographs; paintings by artists of the 1860s; letters from soldiers; newspaper articles; and uniforms, battle flags, and items people used in their day-to-day life. Clip the pictures, articles, and drawings and keep them in the box.

Separate your clippings into subjects. Choose your first subject and start its page in the scrapbook. Sketch a draft layout of the clippings and photographs of the subject. Build the page around the most dramatic or interesting illustration or article. Choose a sheet from your selection of paper for a background and set it on your workspace. Arrange the clippings and images on the page until you are satisfied with the grouping. You might need the ruler to help you center your arrangement. Use a variety of shapes and sizes of items. You could overlap some items or frame an article or illustration with colored paper.

Does your page need a title? You could create a newspaper-style headline on your computer, print it, and cut it out. Or type up and print an appropriate quote from President Lincoln or another Civil War–era person (make sure you use an old-fashioned font). In neat handwriting, you might copy out part of a soldier's letter home or words from one of Lincoln's speeches to add to your page.

Experiment with different types of paper and cloth to add texture to the page. Cut out and arrange borders and other decorative elements (like stars). When you are completely happy with your arrangement, use glue and the glue stick to adhere the items to the page (the glue stick is best for pieces of paper; use glue for heavier items, like scraps of cloth). When complete and dry, slip your page into a clear plastic sleeve, place it in the binder, and get started on your next subject!

Mary had been hurt by criticism when she moved to Washington; the ladies there gossiped that she was ignorant and vulgar, the poor wife of a country lawyer. She was determined to show them that she was a refined lady.

Though Mary wanted badly to make a good impression on the people who visited her White House, when her husband saw the bills he thought people would be appalled. "It would stink in the land," he exclaimed, that so much had been spent, especially during wartime, for "flub dubs for that house!"

The White House wasn't the only thing to undergo change. The whole city of Washington had transformed. More and more soldiers poured in, volunteering for three-year service in the army, until the population of Washington quadrupled. They pitched their tents around the outskirts of the city, marched in its streets, and drilled in vacant lots. The sounds of bugles, drumbeats, and bagpipes filled the air. So did the smell of baking bread, made for the troops all day and night in the basement of the Capitol Building.

The new leader of this growing army was George Brinton McClellan. After the failure at Bull Run, General McDowell was demoted and Lincoln called the bright, young General McClellan to Washington and handed the reins of the eastern army to him. McClellan seemed to be everywhere, riding confident and upright in his saddle, surrounded by laughing officers. He was an engineer, a West Point graduate, and Mexican War veteran who had written a manual on the art of war. McClellan quickly brought organization and order to the thousands of troops milling around Washington. He was the hero of the day, the general who would lead victorious troops into Virginia. Newspapers called him "the man of destiny" and McClellan happily agreed with

Union troops drilling ❖ Library of Congress

THE ART OF THE AFTERNOON VISIT

THE STRICT ETIQUETTE rules of her time determined how Mary Lincoln visited and received visitors. Dressed in their best daytime attire, ladies made formal social calls on each other. Try these social customs to see what a lady's life was like in the 1860s!

WHAT YOU NEED
- Friends (at least 1 visitor, 1 hostess, and 1 servant—but more makes more fun!)
- Scissors
- White textured paper (heavy but not too stiff)
- Ruler
- Black pen
- White gloves
- Fancy hats
- Fancy dish or tray (called the card receiver)
- Purse

Every 1860s-style social call required the perfect calling card to announce a visitor's presence at the hostess's home. Cut the paper into the correct size for a lady's card: 3 by 2¼ inches. In perfect script, write your name in the center, using "Miss" before your name. Write your address in the lower right-hand corner.

The visitor should place her cards in her reticule (purse), put on gloves and hat, and make her way to the hostess's home. Visit only between three and five o'clock in the afternoon (other times are considered rude) and never on Sunday. Don't even think of calling on a gentleman!

The servant should answer the door with the card receiver in hand. The visitor should politely place her calling card on the receiver. The servant will deliver it to the hostess. If she is not home, she will receive the card later and will, according to social custom, be required to return the visit. If she is in, she will decide whether or not to receive her visitor. She may tell her servant to pretend she is not at home or instruct the servant to escort the visitor into the parlor. If asked to invite the visitor in, the servant should usher her into the room and announce her name clearly to the hostess.

The visitor should sit up straight on the edge of a chair and make polite conversation about general topics (like weather or the latest fashions). Stay only 15 to 30 minutes. If another visitor arrives, stay a few minutes then quietly say good-bye, making it clear, however, that it is not her arrival that caused you to leave. Go on to the next hostess's home.

Sometimes, ladies simply dropped off their cards, folded in specific ways, to leave messages for their friends. An upper left corner folded over meant "congratulations." Proper ladies always left such cards after hearing about an engagement or new baby. Condolences were offered by folding the lower left corner. Can you think of other ways to send messages with your calling cards?

Ladies lovingly placed their friends' calling cards into scrapbooks. The cards of especially important people were cherished as keepsakes. The afternoon visits were important to women, whose lives were much more constricted than those of women today. Whether you wear gloves and hats or not when visiting your friends, remember to cherish them—and never pretend you're not at home!

General George McClellan ❖ National Archives

them. Lincoln thought McClellan a little too confident, but hoped that the young general would bring him victories.

Lincoln appointed famous explorer John Charles Fremont to lead the army in the West. General Fremont quickly announced an edict: all slaves belonging to Rebels in the state of Missouri would be seized and declared free. When the president heard this, he was shocked.

It was critical to keep the still-loyal slave states in the Union. Outraged by Fremont's edict, the border states threatened to join the Confederacy. Lincoln ordered Fremont to cancel the edict (later, Fremont was replaced). Lincoln's order pleased the border states but angered abolitionists, who attacked his decision. But even though Lincoln hated slavery, he felt his first responsibility was to save the Union. Fremont's edict threatened it.

It was only the beginning of President Lincoln's many problems with generals. Months went by and McClellan's only move was to send out a reconnaissance mission. The troops he sent met with tragedy at Ball's Bluff, a hill along the Potomac River. There, Colonel Edward D. Baker, a friend so close to the Lincolns they had named their second son after him, was killed in battle. Lincoln cried, stumbling into the street, when he heard the news about Baker. Another dear friend was lost.

Winfield Scott retired and George McClellan became general in chief of the Union army. The ragtag troops camping in Washington were now the Army of the Potomac. They were fit, drilled, and supplied. Yet McClellan insisted they were not ready for battle. His spies, he told the president, said the Rebels greatly outnumbered them. He couldn't possibly fight until he had many thousands more soldiers.

Lincoln wanted to trust his general and gave McClellan the time and men he needed. But as weeks, then months went by, Lincoln became anxious. It was important to strike before the Confederates became too strong, yet McClellan showed no sign of moving. Union troops in Kentucky and Missouri were not advancing either. The war with the Confederacy was at a standstill.

In the meantime, war nearly broke out with Great Britain and France! Southerners James Mason and John Slidell had escaped the blockade and boarded a British ship, the *Trent*, bound for England. They hoped to convince Britain and France to side with the Confederacy. A U.S. ship stopped the British vessel, searched it, and took the two men prisoner. Across the North, people cheered their capture, but Great Britain was furious. Taking the two men from the neutral vessel was a violation of international law. The British ambassador demanded that the men be set free. And if the United States did not apologize, Britain and France would declare war. Britain began to arm and drill its soldiers. One war was enough, Lincoln thought. The prisoners were released and "the Trent Affair" ended quietly.

A friend visiting the White House asked Lincoln how he liked being president of the United States. "You've heard the story, haven't you," Lincoln replied, "about the man who was ridden out of town on a rail, tarred and feathered? Somebody asked him how he liked it, and he said if it wasn't for the honor of the thing, he would much rather walk!" At times, Lincoln felt that way about the presidency. Every day a new crisis appeared at his door.

The Treasury was running out of money. Secretary of War Cameron was accused of incompetence and worse (Lincoln replaced him with Edwin Stanton). Angry congressmen wanted to know when McClellan planned to fight. Newspapers attacked Lincoln as timid and weak. And still, every day, crowds of petitioners lined the White House hallways, eager to gain the president's ear.

Lincoln was courteous to all of his visitors. He welcomed women with poems and challenged tall men to stand up and compare heights (Lincoln almost always won). Many of the visitors were treated to jokes and yarns that became known as "Lincoln stories." "That reminds me of a little story . . ." he would begin.

CONTRABAND

Arms, military supplies, horses, grains—these were materials an army needed in order to fight. Seizing them could cripple an enemy. Such seized materials were defined as "contraband of war." Slaves put to work by the Confederate army to haul supplies and dig ditches were helpful to the South's war efforts, so one Northern general decided they could be seized, just like military supplies. President Lincoln supported that idea by signing an act saying any slaves serving the Confederacy for military purposes could be seized, then freed. Throughout the war, thousands of such slaves risked their lives to flee for the Union lines. There, they were declared free. These former slaves were nicknamed "contrabands."

Sometimes Lincoln told stories to make a point or to change the subject. A friend said that if someone wanted to find out something that Lincoln did not want him to know, Lincoln would talk on and on, telling so many stories and jokes that the visitor would leave laughing and only later ask himself, "Well, what did I find out?" Sometimes Lincoln told jokes to "whistle away the sadness," as the friend put it. It made people laugh during these hard times, and took away his own weariness. And when he wasn't able to grant a person's request, at least, he thought, he could tell the visitor a joke. He was so friendly and

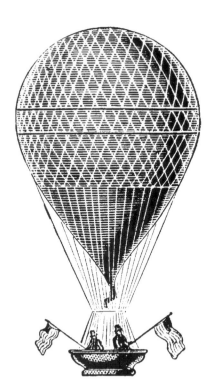

kind to everyone that people began to call him Father Abraham.

Lincoln liked to tell the story about the young soldier heading off to war whose sisters gave him a sash embroidered "Victory or Death." "If it's alright," the soldier said, "I'd prefer one saying 'Victory or Get Hurt Pretty Bad.'" Or the one about the scarecrow that was so frightening that crows brought back corn they'd stolen two years before. He especially liked to make fun of himself. He used to joke that he'd made a promise to himself that "if I ever found a man homelier looking than I was, I would shoot him. Well, I met such a man and said to him 'You had better be settling with your maker and that very quick. I've made an oath to shoot any man homelier than me.' The man replied, 'All I've got to say is that if I'm

worse looking than you are, for God's sake shoot me!'" After telling a joke like that, Lincoln would slap his thigh and laugh as hard as anyone else in the room.

Lincoln's favorite visitors were the inventors who brought gadgets and guns they hoped would be useful in the war effort. A man standing in the hallway with a new rifle in his hands was always welcomed to Lincoln's office, which was soon crammed with weapons. Once, Lincoln experimented with a new gun by firing some practice rounds outside. A sergeant and his men raced up, shouting "Stop!" When they saw who was shooting, they turned and ran in the other direction. Lincoln laughed. "They might have stayed to see the shooting!" he said. He experimented with signal lights from a Washington rooftop and tested gunpowder in his own fireplace. He insisted that the army order new and improved rifles and that the navy try a new design, the ironclad ship. When balloonist Thaddeus Lowe flew above Washington and reported to the president his view of the city and nearby camps, Lincoln persuaded the army to use Lowe's "Balloon Corps" to spy on the Confederate army.

His days were so full, Lincoln barely took time to eat. When he wasn't in his office, he was reviewing troops, meeting with cabinet members, and striding on his long legs to the War Department office to read the latest tele-

PLEASE, JUST CALL ME LINCOLN

Over his lifetime Lincoln's nicknames included Honest Abe, the Rail Splitter, Spotty, the Lone Star of Illinois, the Great Emancipator, Long Abe, and Father Abraham. His secretaries Nicolay and Hay affectionately called him "the Ancient" or "the Tycoon." He preferred, simply, Lincoln.

grams from his generals. When he could get away, he took afternoon carriage rides with Mary or with Secretary of State Seward. At night there were state dinners and receptions, and sometimes quiet evenings with friends, when Lincoln read poems or Shakespeare's plays out loud. Whenever he could, Lincoln went to the theater. He loved plays, especially funny ones, and concerts too. Afterward, he worked and read late into the night.

Just as he had done so many times in his life, Lincoln drove himself to learn. Now he needed to know about military strategy. He studied military manuals, read histories of battles, and pored over the maps in his office. He walked down hallways with plans and reports spilling from his arms.

Lincoln's strategy was to blockade Southern ports and divide the Confederacy by regaining the Mississippi River. At the same time, Northern armies would move into Virginia and Tennessee. Newspapers and the Northern people wanted Richmond, the Confederate capital, captured. But no matter how much the president urged General McClellan to move the troops forward, nothing ever seemed to happen. McClellan, Lincoln said, had "a case of the slows."

General McClellan always had a new reason why his army was not yet ready to fight. He remained convinced that the Confederate army outnumbered his by many thousands. Maybe, he suggested, he would move his army forward in the fall. Lincoln visited McClellan's headquarters, looked at maps, and discussed strategy with him. Fall came and went and still the army did not move. Then McClellan got sick and stayed in bed for three weeks. He insisted he had a plan but refused to tell Lincoln what it was, saying the president couldn't be trusted with the secret. In spite of the general's rudeness, Lincoln said, "I will hold McClellan's horse if he will only bring us success."

President Lincoln reviewing troops

Indiana Historical Society

"The people are impatient," Lincoln finally told a friend. Congress was impatient too. The armies were ready; it was time to fight. The president called a meeting of top generals and told them that "if General McClellan did not want to use the army, I would like to borrow it." Within weeks, Lincoln issued his "General Order No. 1." All forces were to advance forward.

In the meantime, the family celebrated Christmas at the White House with Willie and Tad shooting off firecrackers and pistols. The

White House reception ❧ Library of Congress

president and First Lady welcomed all callers on New Year's Day. Mary planned a grand party for 500 guests to take place a month later, but when her two young boys came down with typhoid fever she thought she should cancel it. The doctor assured her that the boys were in no danger.

The party was a success, with a band playing the "Mary Lincoln Polka" and guests marveling over a sugary replica of a Union fort. But the Lincolns had no heart for celebrating; 12-year-old Willie was growing weaker. Within weeks, their cherished son died, and the White House was draped in black.

While the Lincolns grieved, the war began in earnest. Out in the West, a bold fighter named Ulysses S. Grant captured Confederate forts. McClellan put his army on boats and barges and steamed down the Potomac River with Richmond as his goal. Southern general Thomas J. "Stonewall" Jackson tried to distract those troops from their mission by threatening Washington from the nearby Shenandoah Valley. And in a terrible battle among the peach trees near a country church called Shiloh (Hebrew for "Place of Peace"), Union troops drove Confederate forces back after two bloody days of fighting.

After landing on the Virginia peninsula, McClellan's army moved at a snail's pace. Lincoln thought he would pay a visit to see why. Along with cabinet members Chase and Stanton, he took a boat to the Union base. Once there, he questioned commanders. Norfolk, Virginia, was nearby; Lincoln thought it should be easy enough to capture that Confederate city. The commanders disagreed. It was impossible to land troops close enough to Norfolk to stage an attack, they said.

Late that night, when the moon rose, Lincoln and Stanton climbed into a tugboat and cruised close to the shore, looking for a landing site. Chase kept watch for Confederate troops from another boat while Lincoln landed on Virginia's soil. On his return, Lincoln instructed commanders to land their troops at the spot and attack. The mission succeeded and Norfolk surrendered. "So has ended a brilliant week's campaign of the President," Chase wrote in his diary.

McClellan's campaign eventually brought Union troops so close to Richmond they could hear the city's bells tolling. In a battle outside the city, the leader of the Confederate army fell wounded. He was replaced by Robert E. Lee, the general who had earlier been offered the job of leading the Union army. Without hesitation, Lee threw his men at McClellan's army. The armies clashed for seven days. McClellan retreated, giving up on the attack against Richmond. After many thousands of casualties, the North had made no progress at all.

IN THE HEADLINES

February 1862: Unconditional Surrender! ∽ Brigadier General Ulysses S. Grant moved against Southern forts on the Tennessee and Cumberland rivers, demanding nothing less than "unconditional and immediate surrender." The forts fell and the North rejoiced. Grant received a promotion and a nickname: "Unconditional Surrender Grant."

March 1862: Battle of the Ironclads! ∽ The Confederates covered a captured Union ship with four inches of iron plating and renamed it the *C.S.S. Virginia*. The Virginia crippled three Union ships and threatened the city of Washington before meeting the North's new ironclad, the *U.S.S. Monitor*. The battle was a draw. Both sides claimed victory.

April 1862: McClellan Moves! ∽ General George McClellan's Army of the Potomac moved down the Virginia coast in a great fleet, planning to attack Richmond from an unexpected direction. The army landed, then progressed slowly toward the Confederate capital.

April 1862: Blood Shed in Place of Peace! ∽ The true price of war became obvious after the Battle of Shiloh in Tennessee, with 23,000 men killed, wounded, or captured. The battle was a Northern victory. Still, people complained to Lincoln that Major General U. S. Grant had led his men to slaughter and that he should be removed. "I can't spare this man," said Lincoln, "he fights!"

April 1862: New Orleans Falls! ∽ The city of New Orleans, near the mouth of the Mississippi River, was critical to the Confederacy. It fell into Union hands thanks to David Farragut, who ran his fleet of warships past forts and, with cannons blazing, captured the city. Confederates still controlled the Mississippi River from Vicksburg, Mississippi.

Lincoln called for 300,000 new volunteers. For the moment, he left McClellan in charge of the Army of the Potomac, which soon would return to its camps near Washington. But he took back McClellan's rank of general in chief and gave it to Henry W. Halleck. Halleck, who had written an important book about warfare, was nicknamed "Old Brains." Once in the position, however, Halleck proved to lack boldness and was no more useful, said Lincoln, "than a first-rate clerk." Sadly, brainy Halleck couldn't get the armies moving in the right direction.

Lincoln began to think that the whole war needed a new direction. Ever since the first shots of war, his entire focus had been to save the Union. During that time, many of his visitors pressured him to end slavery, the terrible scourge that had divided the country. Lincoln had always thought that "if slavery is not wrong, then nothing is wrong" but told them that emancipating the slaves was an action he could not take.

Lincoln did not believe that a president had the constitutional right to abolish slavery. Even if he could, he worried that freeing the slaves would send the border slave states flying to join the Confederacy. Losing the border states could mean losing the war and any hope for the Union. He understood, too, that many of those fighting to save the Union might not support the war if it became a war to free the slaves. McClellan had hinted that if the slaves were emancipated, many soldiers would throw down their arms.

But now it was time, as Lincoln said, to "think anew, and act anew." Slavery was like a cancer that had eaten away at the nation. The friction over it had led to this war. There would never be peace between North and South as long as it existed. Even if the states were reunited, the poison of slavery would once again lead to conflict. It wasn't enough to fight for union. It was time to bring an end to slavery.

Even those Northerners who did not want to fight to free slaves would have to agree that there was good reason for doing so. Slave labor helped the Confederate cause. Freeing the slaves in the Rebel states would take away the huge labor force that kept the Confederacy fed and clothed. Freeing the slaves could bring the war closer to an end.

Lincoln had already taken some steps against slavery. He had signed bills to abolish it in Washington, D.C., and in all federal territories. He tried to get the border states to accept compensated emancipation, by which owners would be paid for the value of their freed slaves. Because he thought freed slaves would not be accepted in white communities, Lincoln also talked to black leaders about colonization—sending freed blacks to colonies in Central America or to Liberia in Africa.

Representatives of the border states refused to consider compensated emancipation. Free black people said an even louder "No!" to the idea of colonization. They felt betrayed by the idea, for the United States was their country too. They were born, had labored, and had raised their families in America. They were eager to bear arms and fight. If and when freedom came for slaves, they would stay.

Thousands of "contraband" fugitive slaves had migrated to Washington and its outlying neighborhoods. The Lincolns' cook was a runaway slave. Mary Lincoln's seamstress and friend, Elizabeth Keckley, was a one-time slave who had paid $1,200 for her own freedom. She convinced Mary to give money and assistance to contraband slaves and to help them find jobs.

Almost every summer day, Lincoln rode past a contraband camp of tents and shacks, home to more than 4,000 fugitive slaves. He saw them on his way to and from the Soldiers' Home. Only three miles from the White House, in a quiet country setting, the Soldiers' Home provided shelter for aged and disabled veterans. A cottage on its grounds provided refuge for Lincoln, Mary, and Tad. They moved there during the summers, to get relief from Washington's sweltering heat.

"I see the President almost every day," wrote poet Walt Whitman. Lincoln bowed to the

"Coming into the Lines," sketch by Edwin Forbes

poet from the saddle of his gray horse. During his first summer at the Soldiers' Home, he rode alone to and from work (though on some days, Tad followed behind on his pony). Lincoln's wife and his advisers were appalled. The president could be kidnapped—or worse.

One soldier said he saw Lincoln "bareheaded," galloping into the grounds late one night. When he asked the president what had happened, Lincoln said that a gun had gone off, causing his horse to bolt and his hat to fly off. The soldier retrieved Lincoln's tall hat only to find a bullet hole in its crown. Lincoln asked him to keep the incident quiet.

Soldiers' Home, Washington D.C.

Library of Congress

Lincoln even joked about threats to his life. The first two or three, he said, had made him "a little uncomfortable but there is nothing like getting *used* to things." Eventually a company of soldiers guarded the Lincoln cottage and a cavalry unit accompanied the president on his rides. Poet Whitman could hear their sabers clanking as they rode.

Mary loved their quieter life at the Soldiers' Home. Tad was in heaven. He made friends with the soldiers who camped there and they gave him the title of "Third Lieutenant." Tad rode his pony in their drills and when the soldiers lined up for dinner, he got in line, too.

One summer day, the president shared a carriage ride with two of his cabinet members. To their surprise, he said he had "about come to the conclusion that we must free the slaves or be ourselves subdued." A week later, he announced his plan to his entire cabinet.

Lincoln had found a legal way to end slavery that could keep the border states calm. He would continue to offer compensated emancipation to the border states. And, as a special war measure, he would by military decree free all slaves in the Confederate states. Some of his advisers felt it was too radical a step. One thought it would cost Lincoln the next election. But it was clear that the president meant to free the slaves. Secretary of State Seward had one suggestion—wait. The Union armies needed to win a battle first, he said, or else an emancipation proclamation would seem like "our last shriek on the retreat."

Lincoln agreed to wait for a victory, but at times it felt like that wait would never end. Late at night, he wrote and rewrote his Emancipation Proclamation, changing a word here, adding a line there, then locking it away again in a drawer.

One day, from the lawn of the White House, Lincoln listened anxiously to the boom of artillery. A battle raged only a day's march from Washington on the same ground, near Bull Run Creek, where the first big battle of the war had been fought. A new Union general led this fight: John Pope, who boasted that he had always seen the backs of his enemies. Lincoln spent the night in the War Department's telegraph office, hoping for good news from the battlefield. But once again, Union troops were defeated and forced to withdraw. "We are whipped again," a dejected Lincoln said to his secretary, John Hay.

Southern general Robert E. Lee pressed on, ordering his army to move into the North. When the Confederate troops crossed into Maryland, Lincoln ordered General McClellan to engage them in battle. The armies met at Sharpsburg, along Antietam Creek, in a terrible and bloody battle that ended with a Southern retreat. McClellan, instead of vigorously pursuing Lee's troops to deliver a final blow, let them go.

The Battle of Antietam left many thousands dead or injured. Lee's army had survived and escaped. But it was a victory of sorts. Lincoln honored it by announcing his plan to emancipate the slaves. On January 1, 1863, he would sign his proclamation. After that, all slaves in

The first reading of the Emancipation Proclamation before the cabinet, painting by F. B. Carpenter ❖ Library of Congress

> *"In giving freedom to the slave, we assure freedom to the free — honorable alike in what we give, and what we preserve."*
>
> —Abraham Lincoln, December 1862, message to Congress

FREDERICK DOUGLASS CELEBRATES FREEDOM

"**W**e shout with joy that we live to record this righteous decree!" exclaimed Frederick Douglass when the Emancipation Proclamation was signed. Douglass knew first-hand the cruelty of bondage.

A slave in a Baltimore household, young Frederick watched great ships sail in and out of that city's harbor. He resolved that one day he would be as free as a ship sailing across the sea. He resolved, too, to learn how to read. He gave his food to boys on the street in exchange for help spelling out words.

One day, Frederick disguised himself as a sailor and escaped on a ship sailing to the North. There he became a thundering and eloquent public speaker, wrote a book on his life as a slave, and founded an abolitionist newspaper called *The North Star.* The self-taught man's words reached people around the world.

Douglass's words reached the White House too, where Abraham Lincoln welcomed him and listened to his advice.

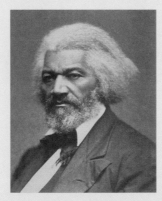

Frederick Douglass
National Archives

the Confederate states would be "then, thenceforward, and forever free."

Many white Northerners objected to the change in the war's aim. They were willing to lay down their lives for the Union, but not for black freedom. George McClellan told his friends he wanted to resign. But many others welcomed the news with gladness, celebrating the announcement with bonfires and processions. One man sent Lincoln six hams! News of the proclamation spread like fire through contraband camps and other black communities. Families rejoiced, knowing that never again would they be separated at an auction block. Black men, who were not allowed to enlist in the army, spoke hopefully of someday joining the fight for freedom. Happy crowds gathered outside the White House to serenade the president.

Proclaiming the end of slavery was one thing, but it would take Union victories to actually free the slaves. Hoping to urge McClellan forward, Lincoln visited the Army of the Potomac at its camp along Antietam Creek. Again, McClellan complained that he needed more troops, more horses, and more supplies before he could pursue the enemy. Accompanied by a friend, Lincoln climbed a hill above the battlefield. He swept his arm before him, asking his friend, "What is all this?" "Why, it's the Army of the Potomac," his friend replied. "No," said Lincoln, "this is General McClellan's bodyguard."

Back in Washington, after receiving more letters of complaint from McClellan, Lincoln reached the end of his patience with "Tardy George." It was clear that this general could never lead the North to victory. It was time for a new commander. Lincoln ordered McClellan to immediately turn over his command to Major General Ambrose Burnside.

Burnside, tall and imposing, sported magnificent whiskers that inspired a new word—"sideburns." Though reluctant to take command of the army, once in charge he moved into action. He hoped to march his troops right into the Confederate capital of Richmond. That plan changed when his army faced Robert E. Lee's in a terrible battle at Fredericksburg, Virginia. The battle turned into a dreadful slaughter in which wave after wave of Union soldiers fell.

Over the next months, Union and Confederate forces clashed on many fronts. Armies fought in Corinth, Mississippi, at Perryville, Kentucky, and along Stones River in Tennessee. In Missouri, small bands skirmished. Ulysses S. Grant struggled yet couldn't seem to take Vicksburg, the last Confederate stronghold on the Mississippi River. In Washington, Lincoln's own advisers also warred with each other. Lincoln grew increasingly pale and stooped by his worries. Everything was going wrong. But

President Lincoln and General McClellan at Antietam ❖ National Archives

he felt sure of one thing. He did not once doubt his decision to emancipate the slaves.

On New Year's morning the Lincolns held a reception, opening the White House doors to all visitors. For hours, the president shook hands with each and every caller. In the afternoon, he sat down at his desk to sign the Emancipation Proclamation. Lincoln picked up a pen, then put it down again. After shaking hands with people all morning, his hand trembled. He told those who had gathered for

"WHEREAS . . .":
AN EXCERPT FROM LINCOLN'S EMANCIPATION PROCLAMATION

"**Whereas,** on the twenty-second day of September, in the year of our Lord one thousand eight hundred and sixty-two, a proclamation was issued by the President of the United States, containing, among other things, the following, to wit:

'That on the first day of January, in the year of our Lord one thousand eight hundred and sixty-three, all persons held as slaves within any State or designated part of a State, the people whereof shall then be in rebellion against the United States, shall be then, thenceforward, and forever free; and the Executive Government of the United States, including the military and naval authority thereof, will recognize and maintain the freedom of such persons, and will do no act or acts to repress such persons, or any of them, in any efforts they may make for their actual freedom.'"

Reading the Emancipation Proclamation
❖ Indiana Historical Society

this historic moment that he did not want people in the future to think he was hesitant and trembling when he signed the Emancipation Proclamation. He picked up the pen again. "Abraham Lincoln," he wrote, as carefully as when he first learned to sign his name.

President Lincoln in 1864, photographed by Mathew Brady ❖ Library of Congress

THE SIGNING of the Emancipation Proclamation gave hope to millions of enslaved people. Their story—from capture in Africa to backbreaking labor, forced separation of families, and desperate midnight flights—could end with freedom for them and their children.

Use collage, in the form of a quilt, to tell the story of American slavery. Why a quilt? For the "safe quilts," with secret codes stitched into their patterns, that were once hung outside homes along the Underground Railroad.

WHAT YOU NEED

- ▨ Notebook
- ▨ Pencil
- ▨ 30 sheets (approximately) of construction paper in a mix of colors
- ▨ Ruler
- ▨ Scissors
- ▨ Scraps of paper in different patterns and textures
- ▨ White glue
- ▨ 22-by-28-inch poster board
- ▨ Heavy books

Plan your design in your notebook. The collage here shows 12 scenes, including the continent of Africa, a runaway slave, Dred Scott, and black soldiers marching off to fight. You might choose other scenes and people: a slave market, the book *Uncle Tom's Cabin*, Harriet Tubman, or Frederick Douglass. Sketch each scene.

Pick out 12 sheets of construction paper in your favorite colors. Using ruler and pencil, draw a 6-by-6-inch square on each. Cut the squares out.

Start with the first scene. In pencil, lightly draw the elements of the scene onto pieces of construction paper and colored scrap paper. Cut out the pieces of paper. Arrange the papers on the square before gluing. When you're satisfied with the way it looks, pick up each piece and put a small amount of glue on the back, then stick it in place on its square. Repeat for each square.

Arrange the 12 squares evenly on the poster board, then glue into place. Carefully put some heavy books on top of the poster and let them sit for a few hours to flatten the collage.

"INCREASED DEVOTION"

"**M**y God! What will the country say?" Lincoln groaned. The news from Virginia could not have been worse. Lee's Rebels, though outnumbered two to one, had crushed the Northern army on the battleground of Chancellorsville. Union casualties soared to over 17,000 men. People across the North would soon frantically scan newspaper lists for names of beloved sons and husbands killed or wounded in battle. "What will the country say?"

The country had already said plenty over the past few months. Death and suffering had touched nearly every family. After the last big defeat, at Fredericksburg, General Burnside tried to move

his troops around the Rebel forces to attack from the rear. His army was defeated—not by the enemy, but by a torrential rainstorm. With men, horses, and carriages mired in the mud, the advance came to a soggy halt. Newspapers mocked the "Mud March" and blamed Lincoln for the army's failures.

Out in the West, after months of struggle, General Grant's efforts to take Vicksburg, Mississippi, seemed mired too. He tried to dig a canal to bypass the city. He sent soldiers and sailors down back roads and little creeks on failed surprise attacks. Nothing worked. People urged Lincoln to get rid of Grant, some suggesting that the general was a drunk.

Lincoln refused to fire Grant, but he relieved Burnside of his command. Still looking for a commander who could win, Lincoln took a chance on the ambitious and confident Joseph Hooker, a general who had shown promise at the battles of Antietam and Fredericksburg. "Fighting Joe" Hooker boasted that he would soon get the best of "Bobby Lee." The president hoped that was true. "Go forward, and give us victories," he wrote to his new commander.

Hospitals were full. Young men were crippled, imprisoned, dead on the battlefield, or missing in action. The country was weary of failure and sacrifice, weary of war, weary of

"Stuck in the Mud," sketch by Edwin Forbes

Lincoln's calls for new troops to fill the places of those who had died. Some objected to the Emancipation Proclamation and turned against Lincoln. Even former supporters were unhappy with the way the president ran the war. Many suggested it was time to make peace with the Confederacy, either recognizing it as a separate nation or restoring the Union as it once was, with slavery intact. Lincoln refused to consider giving up on the Union or going back on his promise to free the slaves. "I am a slow walker but I never walk back," he said.

Rumors spread that Northern Rebel sympathizers—called Copperheads (after a type of venomous snake)—were plotting to overthrow the government. In some Northern states, people threatened to break away from the Union just as the Confederacy had.

Lincoln, too, was weary. He told an acquaintance that it was a great irony that he, who hated violence and "sickened at the sight of blood" should be "cast in the middle of a great civil war." He grew thin and pale, and his wrinkles deepened. His shoulders slumped under the great burdens he carried. Yet there was no time for rest. He worked day and night, skipping meals and sleeping on the couch in the telegraph office.

Though swamped with work, Lincoln continued to open his door to visitors. More and more, they were widows seeking help or

HABEAS CORPUS: "YOU HAVE THE BODY"

Spies in the North sent coded messages to Confederate leaders. Rebel sympathizers smuggled weapons and medicine to the South. Union soldiers home on leave were threatened, even killed. To stop this "fire in the rear," as Lincoln called it, the president suspended the writ of habeas corpus. This meant that anyone suspected of aiding the Rebel cause could be arrested by military officials and either held without trial or tried in a military court.

A writ (order) of habeas corpus (Latin for "you have the body") is an order from a judge demanding that the body (the person arrested) be brought to court so the judge can make sure the arrest was legal. As an emergency measure, Lincoln suspended that basic legal protection and Congress voted to support him. Thousands of civilians were arrested.

Most of those arrested were in the border states, where loyalties—and often families—were divided. They had attacked Union soldiers or destroyed supplies. Many were spies. But others had simply spoken out against the government, like former Ohio congressman Clement L. Vallandigham. Vallandigham made speeches against "King Lincoln" and the war. He was arrested and banished to the Confederacy.

Many protested the writ's suspension, calling Lincoln a tyrant and a despot. Lincoln said that with spies and Rebel sympathizers at large, the country was in danger. He pointed to the Constitution, which stated that the writ could be suspended "when in cases of rebellion or invasion the public safety may require it."

Protection of personal liberty is a basic American right. Yet during the Civil War, the very existence of the nation was at stake. If you were president, what would you do?

people looking for word of sons and brothers fighting the war. Others came requesting mercy for deserters (soldiers who had fled from military service) who now faced the penalty of execution. Lincoln called these his "leg cases," and said they could not help it if their legs ran from battle. He granted pardons to nearly all of them.

One of Lincoln's few pleasures was visiting soldiers in the forts surrounding Washington. He felt at ease around the soldiers and enjoyed their company. He shared coffee with them, or a plate of beans. The soldiers, in return, loved "Old Abe"; they smiled to see his long legs dangling nearly to the ground as he rode his horse. When Lincoln visited General Hooker and the Army of the Potomac at their camp in Virginia, the soldiers cheered and honored him with 21-gun salutes.

Visiting the army camp was a welcome relief from the burdens of Washington. Mary and Tad joined Lincoln on the trip and the family made camp in a tent next to General Hooker's. Each day the army put on a grand review for the president. Trumpets blared and drums rolled. Infantrymen marched in step and cavalry horses pranced. Tad was thrilled. He ran through the camp, inspecting all the tents and chatting merrily with the soldiers.

Just across the river, Confederate soldiers guarded the nearby town of Fredericksburg. Lincoln borrowed a field glass and squinted through it to get a close look. A Rebel soldier standing guard saw the tall man in the stovepipe hat and recognized him as the Union

WHAT'S GOING ON?

Thanks to television news, cell phones, and Internet access, we speed along on the "information superhighway." Back in Lincoln's time, it was more like a faint trail through a dark forest. Days after great battles were fought, the president still might not know who had won. Handwritten letters from his generals were carried to him by messengers on boats, trains, or horseback. Other news came from traveling eyewitnesses, or Lincoln read it in the newspaper just like everyone else. Sometimes he looked for news in Confederate newspapers. One day as Lincoln rode his horse to the Soldiers' Home, he met with carriages carrying wounded soldiers. He rode alongside them, asking eagerly for news of the battle they had fought.

But thanks to the telegraph, Lincoln wasn't always in the dark. A relatively new invention, the telegraph became a vital tool during the Civil War. Lincoln recognized its importance and, by military order, took over the nation's telegraph lines. Nearly 10,000 operators sent coded messages to Washington and military camps across the country. Dot-and-dash messages sped along miles of wire to the War Department's telegraph office. There, a sleepy Lincoln rose from the couch to receive the latest news.

Army Signal and Telegraph

MORSE CODE (named for its 1844 inventor, Samuel Morse) is a system of short pulses ("dots"), long pulses ("dashes"), and the pauses between them that was used to send messages along telegraph wires. Though it was high-tech in the 1860s, today the telegraph is defunct. But you can still use Morse code to send secret messages to your friends! You can dot-and-dash on paper or with flashing lights or sound. Try it different ways!

WHAT YOU NEED

- A friend
- 2 copies of the Morse code
- Paper
- Pencil
- 2 flashlights

Make two copies of the Morse code from this page, give one to a friend, and spend some time memorizing it. A good way to do this is to keep a copy in your pocket and practice with it every day. Whenever you see an ad or a sign, pull out the code and spell out the words in dots and dashes.

Ready to communicate in code? Try it with flashlights in a dark room. A one-second on-and-off of the flashlight will stand for a dot. For a dash, turn the flashlight on for three seconds, then turn it off. Leave one second of darkness between each letter. Words should be separated by seven seconds of darkness. Now turn off the lights and say "Hi." The letter "H" is four dots (four one-second on-and-off flashes of light). Leave one second of darkness then go on to the letter "i," represented by two dots (two on-and-off flashes of light).

Turn on the lights and try Morse code in sound. Use your voice to sound out quick dots or longer dashes. "Di-di-di-di," pause, then "di-di," and you've said "Hi" with sound. Make a three-second sound for a dash—"daaaah." Again, leave one second between letters and seven seconds between words.

Using light or sound, send a message to your friend. He or she can jot down the message as you send it, then decode it. Take turns sending and receiving. Or you can make it a game with several players. Send a message and see who can decode it the fastest.

Want to receive a Morse code e-mail? Send any message to telegraph@janisherbertforkids.com!

MORSE CODE

| DOT (·) = 1 second pulse | | Leave 1 second interval between letters. |
| DASH (—) = 3 second pulse | | Leave 7 second interval between words. |

A	·—	G	——·	M	——	S	···	Y	—·——
B	—···	H	····	N	—·	T	—	Z	——··
C	—·—·	I	··	O	———	U	··—		
D	—··	J	·———	P	·——·	V	···—		
E	·	K	—·—	Q	——·—	W	·——		
F	··—·	L	·—··	R	·—·	X	—··—		

president. He took off his own cap and made a gentlemanly bow to Lincoln.

Before leaving the camp, Lincoln visited the army's hospital tents. He moved from bed to bed with a kind word for each wounded soldier. Lincoln knew and appreciated the sacrifices these men had made. Mary, too, spent time visiting army hospitals. Emotional and sensitive, she jumped when a door slammed, but she found the strength to sit by the bedside of sick and mangled soldiers. She brought them flowers and wrote letters home for them. She let her kind deeds go unnoticed, never bringing journalists along on her visits.

Mary's kindnesses were overlooked, but her failings got plenty of attention. She had few friends in Washington. Fiercely devoted to her husband, she refused to speak to those who criticized him. She was jealous, too, of anyone who gained his attention. People gossiped about her bad temper and her famous shopping sprees. Mary found comfort in possessions, and especially needed comfort after Willie's death. Shopping became an obsession. In one four-month period, she bought 300 pairs of gloves.

Because she was from Kentucky, Southerners called Mary a traitor. Because her four brothers and three brothers-in-law all joined the Confederate army, Northerners whispered that she was a Rebel sympathizer. When she invited her sister, a Confederate widow, to stay at the White House, Mary scandalized Washington. Still heartbroken by Willie's death, she found little comfort anywhere.

Willie's death brought Lincoln even closer to his son Tad. Little Tad adored his father, whom he called "Papa-Day." The two read together and played checkers. Lincoln helped

Hospitalized Union soldiers ❖ National Archives

his son train his little puppy. Many nights, while his father worked late, Tad slept on the couch in Lincoln's office.

With support fading and recruitment down, Lincoln signed a new law. For the first time, the federal government could draft men into the army. Men between 20 and 45 were eligible for the draft, but those who had the money could pay $300 to get out of serving or buy substitutes to serve in their place. Many cried that this made it "a rich man's war but a poor man's fight!" Antidraft riots broke out in Northern cities. In New York City, angry mobs burned buildings and black neighborhoods, killing more than 100 people during a four-day riot.

There was one group of men eager to fight. "The black man!" said abolitionist and one-time slave Frederick Douglass. "Can he not wield a sword, fire a gun, march and counter-march, and obey orders like any other?" Lincoln, who earlier thought that arming blacks would outrage the people of the border states, finally agreed.

Douglass worked to recruit black soldiers for the Union army—two of his own sons signed up to serve. Northern freedmen lined up to enlist; Southern slaves made their way to Union lines to join the fight for freedom. Their military service, and that of any white officers who led them, came with added danger. The

Lincoln and his son Tad ❖ Library of Congress

PLAY "FOLLOWINGS"

PEOPLE OFTEN saw Lincoln and his son Tad walking along a gravel path, throwing pebbles in a game called "Followings." Their game always began at the White House and ended at the steps of the War Department.

WHAT YOU NEED
▦ Rocks or marbles   ▦ 2 players

This is a game to play while you're on your way somewhere (but not in a hurry!). The first player should throw his or her rock in the direction of travel. The second player throws his or her rock at the first player's rock. If player 2 hits the first rock, he or she gets a point and a chance to throw and try to hit the first rock again. Player

2 keeps throwing and getting points until he or she misses.

Walk up to the place where the first rock landed, then trade places by letting player 2 throw first. Player 1 has a chance to try to hit the other player's rock and gain some points. The game continues until the destination is reached.

few weeks a nurse watched over her day and night. Many thought the carriage had been sabotaged in an attempt on the president's life.

For three days, the armies struggled on the fields and hills surrounding Gettysburg. Fierce battles raged for possession of Culp's Hill, Round Top, Little Round Top, and Cemetery Ridge. Men bled and died in peach orchards and wheat fields. Then, on the Fourth of July, after losing more than one-third of his army, Lee withdrew his troops. Gettysburg's casualties numbered a staggering 53,000 men.

"Going into Action," sketch made at Gettysburg by Edwin Forbes

Though the battle was a Northern victory, Lincoln despaired when General Meade wrote him that "the invader" was "driven from our soil." "The whole country is our soil!" Lincoln exclaimed. He wanted this terrible war brought to an end, but Lee's troops had been allowed to retreat to the Virginia side of the Potomac River, where they would recover and soon be ready to fight again. "We had them within our grasp!" Lincoln despaired.

Still, the president was grateful for the hard-fought victory at Gettysburg. And only days later, more good news arrived. Out in the West, General Grant had won battles across Mississippi and had captured its capital, Jackson. On the Fourth of July, as Lee withdrew from Gettysburg, the Confederate stronghold of Vicksburg surrendered to Grant. "Grant is my man and I am his for the rest of the war!" said Lincoln. With Vicksburg's surrender, the Union took control of the Mississippi River, cutting the Confederacy in two. No longer could Confederate guns stop Union boats and supply vessels as they navigated the river. Happy Washingtonians gathered outside the White House to serenade the president.

Mary, recovered from her carriage accident, spent the rest of that summer in cool New Hampshire with sons Robert and Tad. Lincoln worked at the White House and spent his summer nights at their cottage at the Soldiers'

Home. "My dear Wife," he wrote to Mary, "All is well." The only bad news Lincoln reported was about Tad's goat Nanny. "The day you left," he wrote, "Nanny was found resting herself, and chewing her little cud, on the middle of Tad's bed." Lincoln was sad to report that she had then disappeared.

Some nights, Lincoln walked outside to join in the talk at the soldiers' camp. One night he and secretary John Hay rode to the Naval Observatory to view the moon and stars through a new telescope. Lincoln spent evenings reciting poetry and telling jokes to visitors. Hay's eyes drifted shut as the president read aloud from Shakespeare's plays.

One night a messenger woke the president with bad news. Union forces had been routed in battle at Chickamauga, Tennessee, and had made a messy retreat to Chattanooga. It was a terrible loss under a confused and stunned general who acted, Lincoln said, "like a duck hit on the head." Though he had great confidence in the brave men of his armies, Lincoln despaired of his generals. For the last few long weeks, Meade had kept the Army of the Potomac in camp, showing no inclination to go after Lee's army. "What can I do with such generals as we have?" Lincoln asked.

There was one general in whom Lincoln had confidence. He ordered Ulysses S. Grant to take command of all the western armies.

Though on crutches at the time, Grant immediately headed for besieged Chattanooga. Wending his way over a dangerous mountain road, on train, on horseback, and even on the backs of his men, Grant avoided enemy fire. Inside the city, starving Union soldiers stared at the Rebel guns. Under Grant's leadership, the men cried, "Remember Chickamauga!" and defeated the Southern troops who surrounded them.

"The Father of Waters again goes unvexed to the sea."
—Abraham Lincoln

Chickamauga. Chancellorsville. Fredericksburg. Antietam. There had been so many battles and so many soldiers who had sacrificed their lives. Lincoln rarely left Washington during his presidency, but when he was invited to speak at a dedication for a soldiers' cemetery, he gladly accepted the chance to honor the men. He wrote most of his speech, tucked the pages inside his hat, and boarded a train for Gettysburg.

Thousands of people had gathered in Gettysburg for the dedication ceremony. Crowds serenaded outside the window of the home where Lincoln stayed that night. He sat up late to put the finishing touches on his speech, and in the morning he inspected the battleground with Secretary of State Seward. Its fields were still littered with knapsacks and cartridge boxes. Horse carcasses and stacks of coffins bore witness to that summer's terrible battle.

As Lincoln rode past lines of saluting soldiers toward the speaking platform, a single cannon fired once every minute. Military bands played while the crowd gathered. Lincoln's speech was not the main attraction for them that day. People were more eager to hear the famous speaker Edward Everett.

In his two-hour speech, Everett eloquently described the three-day battle of Gettysburg. Many in the audience cried as he recounted the events that occurred on the very fields where they stood. When Lincoln rose to give his speech, they shifted, wiped their eyes, and settled in for the next long oration.

Lincoln put on his reading glasses and took his speech from his coat pocket. "Four score and seven years ago . . ." he began. In just over two minutes, he completed his speech.

Lincoln at Gettysburg ❖ Library of Congress

Lincoln's address was so short that it was over before some even realized that he had begun.

Lincoln feared his address was a failure. "That speech won't scour," he told a friend, using an old phrase from his farming days. He meant his speech was like a plow so caked with soil that it could not till the earth. Many would disagree. One newspaper said that his remarks would "live among the annals of man."

Back in Washington, Lincoln came down with a mild case of smallpox and took to his bed for three weeks. He joked, saying of the swarm of people who still demanded favors from him, "Now I have something I can give to them all!"

Even from his sickbed, the president continued to work. The recent victories gave Lincoln hope that the end of the war was in sight. When that day came, what would be the best way to restore the Southern states to the Union? It was time to think of ways to reconstruct the nation. Lincoln wrote a proclamation that would grant full pardons to those Confederates who swore an oath to protect the Constitution and the Union. After one-tenth of the voters of a Rebel state took this oath, their state, with Congress's approval, could once again become part of the United States.

The year was drawing to a close. In winter camps, soldiers built huts and huddled around campfires. At the White House, Tad

THE GETTYSBURG ADDRESS

"**Four score** and seven years ago our fathers brought forth on this continent, a new nation, conceived in Liberty, and dedicated to the proposition that all men are created equal.

"Now we are engaged in a great civil war, testing whether that nation, or any nation, so conceived and so dedicated, can long endure. We are met on a great battle-field of that war. We have come to dedicate a portion of that field, as a final resting place for those who here gave their lives that that nation might live. It is altogether fitting and proper that we should do this.

"But, in a larger sense, we can not dedicate—we can not consecrate—we can not hallow—this ground. The brave men, living and dead, who struggled here, have consecrated it, far above our poor power

Soldiers' monument at Gettysburg

❧ Gettysburg National Military Park

to add or detract. The world will little note, nor long remember what we say here, but it can never forget what they did here. It is for us the living, rather, to be dedicated here to the unfinished work which they who fought here have thus far so nobly advanced. It is rather for us to be here dedicated to the great task remaining before us—that from these honored dead we take increased devotion to that cause for which they gave the last full measure of devotion—that we here highly resolve that these dead shall not have died in vain—that this nation, under God, shall have a new birth of freedom—and that government of the people, by the people, for the people, shall not perish from the earth."

DO YOU SUFFER FROM GLOSSOPHOBIA? Not fear of lip gloss—it's fear of public speaking! Many people do, but a few tips will help you overcome your nervousness and enjoy giving a speech.

WHAT YOU NEED
- Index cards
- Podium
- Audience

Whether a speech is about politics or platypuses, you want it to captivate your audience. A memorable speech has a strong opening, a main body that outlines its points concisely, and an ending that inspires. Study the Gettysburg Address, and other famous speeches like Martin Luther King Jr.'s "I have a dream" speech or John F. Kennedy's inaugural speech (see "Web Sites to Explore" at the end of the book for a site dedicated to great speeches). Can you pick out the goals of the speakers? What are their main points? How do their endings convince or inspire?

For this activity, you can write your own speech or memorize the Gettysburg Address. Write down the main points of your speech on index cards. If you lose track of your place while speaking, you can quickly refer to your outline.

Because even a well-written speech can fall flat if delivered badly, your voice and body language are critical. A reporter who witnessed Lincoln's inspiring Cooper Institute speech said Lincoln's tones, gestures, and connection with the audience were indescribable. Your voice and inflection can keep people on the edge of their seats. Your body language will tell them you are sincere and passionate about your subject.

Before you give your speech, become familiar with the room so you are comfortable with the setting. Before you get on stage, go for a long walk or get some exercise. Do some pre-fidgeting—give yourself a good shake. Visualize yourself giving a successful speech, and the audience cheering.

When you step in front of the audience, hold yourself confidently. Keep your shoulders comfortably back and breathe normally. Keep your hands out of your pockets and gesture with them naturally. Most important, make eye contact with your listeners.

Remember as you look at them that the audience wants to hear what you have to say, and that they want you to succeed.

When you speak, pronounce each word clearly. Nervous people tend to speak too quickly—take your time and speak slowly. A good pause is often very effective in a speech. If you want to emphasize a word or phrase, pause for a moment before saying it (Lincoln often did). Avoid slurring your words. Avoid "ums" and "you-knows." And avoid speaking in monotone (it puts people to sleep). Vary your pitch, and when you reach a peak in your speech, raise the volume of your voice.

The best thing you can do to be an effective speaker is to think about the message you are delivering instead of yourself. If you are passionate about your subject, you will be excited about sharing it with people.

Statue from Lincoln's tomb
❖ Photograph by Tim Ross

begged his father to spare the Christmas turkey. ("He's a good turkey and I don't want him killed!" cried Tad. Lincoln wrote the bird a reprieve.) Cannons boomed around Washington as a statue representing freedom was lifted to the top of the newly completed Capitol Building dome. Days later, inside the building, members of Congress listened to Lincoln's plan to reconstruct the warring states. The president was looking toward the future and a Union restored.

"WHAT WE SAY HERE..."

Despite his lack of formal education, Lincoln's writings and speeches are considered the greatest of any of the American presidents. Writer Harriet Beecher Stowe thought Lincoln's words were so profound they should be etched in gold. The Gettysburg Address is one of the best speeches ever made, and has become one of the best known.

How did Lincoln become a great writer? He read and learned from great, classic works. He studied grammar. He chose words carefully so they expressed exactly what he meant to say. He often read out loud, a practice that gave him a sense of how words sounded. When he wrote a speech, he wrote it for the ear.

What makes the Gettysburg Address a great speech? Lincoln chose short words to give the speech its strength. He used words that rhyme ("Four score") or that start with the same sound ("new nation"), because such words are pleasing to the ear. Also pleasing is the way he used repetition in phrases like "we can not dedicate—we can not consecrate—we can not hallow," or "government of the people, by the people, for the people."

It is remarkable that the Gettysburg Address makes no reference to the specifics of the battle, to the Emancipation Proclamation, or to the differences of North and South. Lincoln's speech rose above the particulars of that day. Instead of describing the battle or making political points, Lincoln stood at Gettysburg to redefine the nation and give meaning to its suffering—all in 272 simple and stirring words.

"WITH MALICE TOWARD NONE"

The Army of the Potomac marched into the dark, tangled Virginia forest known as the Wilderness. Lincoln's hopes for victory and a restored Union went with them. For three anxious days, he heard nothing as the Union troops met Lee's Army of Northern Virginia in deadly combat.

Leading the Union troops was newly appointed general in chief Ulysses S. Grant. After three years of pushing reluctant generals forward, Lincoln had finally found one who would fight. Grant had accepted his commission in a brief visit to the White House. People crowded to see this general who won battles, standing on tables to get a better look at the quiet officer in the wrinkled uniform.

When Lincoln finally heard the news from the battlefield, he was devastated. The terrible battle in the Wilderness had ended with a Union defeat. The dense forests of the Wilderness had caught fire. Wounded soldiers caught in the flames cried for help. The usually stoic Grant wept at the suffering, then ordered his forces to prepare for a march. "Another ske-

A NEW COMMANDER

From the first shots of war, the army's generals had frustrated Lincoln. The promising General McClellan loved to command but hated to fight. When boastful General Hooker claimed victory before battle, Lincoln suggested he be more like a hen, who "never cackles until the egg is laid." General Burnside was a reluctant leader; General Meade failed to follow through on the victory at Gettysburg.

Ulysses S. Grant, hero of Vicksburg and Chattanooga, cared little for fanfare and ceremony. His uniform was often dusty and wrinkled (but his horse always perfectly groomed). He chewed unlit cigars and, tone deaf, claimed to recognize only two songs—one was "Yankee Doodle," and the other wasn't.

Early in the war, after Grant conquered two Confederate forts, people joked that his initials stood for "Unconditional Surrender." Actually, Grant's real name was Hiram Ulysses. A clerk once mistakenly wrote his name as "Ulysses Simpson"; indifferent to the mistake, Grant never corrected the error. As a general, he was single-minded and aggressive. One soldier said he always looked as if he was determined to "drive his head through a brick wall." Lincoln promoted Grant to lieutenant general and made him general in chief of the Union armies. Grant took command and told the president, "There will be no turning back."

daddle," many thought, another retreat after a licking by General Lee. But their new commander would not turn back.

Time after time, the armies clashed. They struggled desperately in driving rain at a Virginia crossroads called Spotsylvania Courthouse. One Union soldier said that the next battle, at Cold Harbor, was like a dreadful storm of iron and lead. Grant continued to drive the army forward. Men fought and died in numbers that shocked the nation.

Over six awful weeks, the Northern army suffered nearly 60,000 casualties. The dead were hastily buried. The wounded were sent on barges back to Washington, where horse-drawn ambulances met them at the city's wharves. "Grant is a butcher!" Mary Lincoln cried. Many Northerners agreed and called for the general's removal. The president found the suffering nearly unbearable, but he stood by his general.

As the wounded soldiers were brought, groaning, to makeshift hospitals, army reinforcements marched through Washington's streets on their way to the battlefront. Earlier that year, Lincoln had called for 500,000 new recruits. The next month he sent out a call for 200,000. After this latest deadly series of battles, he asked for another 500,000 Northern men to fight. He would send Grant every man he could to end this war. Among them were new black troops who marched briskly to drum rolls and music, and cheered heartily when they saw President Lincoln.

Robert Todd Lincoln was one of the new soldiers. Having just graduated from college, he was eager to join the army. Mary fought against the idea of sending her son to war. She still felt the pain of Willie's death. "Many a poor mother, Mary, has had to make this sacrifice," Lincoln told his wife. "Our son is not more dear to us than the sons of other people are to their mothers." Robert left to serve with General Grant's staff.

Lincoln spent sleepless nights in the telegraph office while the Army of the Potomac fought and marched its way to Petersburg, Virginia. If Grant and his troops could capture Petersburg, a critical railroad junction, then they could take the nearby Confederate capital of Richmond too.

While Grant's soldiers dug fortifications around Petersburg and settled in for a siege, another Union army fought its way toward Atlanta, Georgia. Its commander was the high-strung, redheaded William Tecumseh Sherman. Sherman's men menaced Confederate troops from right and left. The Confederates moved back from Tennessee toward Atlanta, then stalled outside the city.

All the optimism that Lincoln felt earlier had fallen away. Both armies were at a standstill. It began to seem as if the war would never end. The Northern people were "wild for peace," Lincoln's advisers said, ready to sacrifice emancipation and their hopes for a restored Union—anything for an end to war.

Things looked even more hopeless when, late one night, the Lincolns were startled awake by a loud knock on the door of their Soldiers' Home cottage. Secretary of War Stanton urged the family to return immediately to the White House. The Rebels were only miles from the Soldiers' Home. The president was in danger.

Southern general Jubal Early had moved north with 15,000 troops. As they defeated Northern forces in the nearby Shenandoah Valley, Washingtonians grew nervous. Anx-

ious farmers drove their cattle into town; dusty roads were choked with fleeing residents. Early's troops advanced, cutting Washington's rail and telegraph lines. Now they threatened to take Fort Stevens, one of the forts that protected the city.

As the days passed, people huddled in their homes, listening for gunfire. There were few soldiers to defend them; the city had been emptied of troops to fill Grant's ranks. Department clerks grabbed weapons and marched to the forts. Wounded soldiers from the city's hospitals joined them.

Impatient for news, Lincoln left the White House to check the city's defenses. He climbed the parapet of Fort Stevens and stood to look at Early's troops. With his tall hat, he made a fine target for enemy fire. A nearby soldier yelled to him, "Get down, you fool, before you get shot!" and Lincoln smiled and obeyed. But later he climbed up again to watch the skirmishing troops. He badly wanted a victory over the Southern invaders. Men shouted and fought on the fields below. Bullets whizzed by the president. Only when the man standing next to him fell wounded in the leg did Lincoln climb down to safety.

For a time it seemed that all was lost and that Washington would fall to the Southern troops. Then, just at the last moment, reinforcements arrived from Grant's army. The Rebels retreated and Washington was saved. But the invasion had shaken the Northern people, and Early's forces still threatened from the Shenandoah Valley.

With the war going so badly, Lincoln's re-election was threatened too. The presidential election was only months away and hope for victory at its lowest. Lost battles, prolonged sieges, and long casualty lists had taken their toll. Congress fought against Lincoln's plans to reconstruct the nation. Newspaper articles claimed Lincoln was too weak to lead the country to victory. Many people felt it was time to recognize the Southern states as a separate nation, something to which Lincoln would never agree.

In spite of all the troubles, Lincoln was once again nominated by his party, with Andrew Johnson chosen to run as vice president. A self-educated former tailor, Johnson had been a senator from Tennessee when war broke out. When Tennessee seceded, he refused to leave his Senate seat and the Union.

Lincoln's rival in the presidential election was the popular one-time general George McClellan. He promised a Union restored, with slavery intact. Lincoln worried that all the soldiers would vote for their former commander. He told a friend, "I am going to be beaten and, unless some great change takes place, *badly beaten*."

Lincoln's prediction seemed certain as over the long months, casualties mounted and the war's progress stalled. Then one day a triumphant telegram arrived from General Sherman. "Atlanta is ours and fairly won," Sherman declared. Lincoln rejoiced at the news. More good news came from the Gulf of Mexico. Shouting, "Damn the torpedoes! Full speed ahead!" Admiral David Farragut had taken Mobile Bay, the last Gulf port open to Confederate ships. Then a victory in the nearby Shenandoah Valley removed the threat of further raids by Southern troops. The Northern people had new hope.

On Election Day, Lincoln watched as lines of soldiers voted at a nearby polling place. Tad's pet turkey roamed among them. Lincoln joked with his son that perhaps the bird would vote for him. Tad teased back, saying his turkey was not yet old enough to vote. As the votes were counted and the first returns arrived, it became clear that Lincoln did not need the extra help. He sent the good news on to Mary, saying, "She is more anxious than I."

Lincoln won the election handily, thanks in good part to the Union soldiers, who voted overwhelmingly for their Father Abraham. That night, cheering crowds celebrated outside the White House. Inside, Lincoln's old friend Ward Lamon, armed with pistols and bowie knives, slept on the floor outside the president's bedroom. Lamon worried about the rumors and whispers spreading through town. If the president was reelected, some said, he would be assassinated.

With the election won, Lincoln pressed forward with his great work. He realized his Emancipation Proclamation was only a war measure and would expire at war's end. With that in mind, he worked with Congress to pass a constitutional amendment that would outlaw slavery forever.

MAKING AMENDMENTS

Changing the Constitution, the document that defines the United States government, is no small matter. Since its 1788 passage, only 27 amendments have been made. The first 10, known as the Bill of Rights, passed in 1791. Two others passed before Lincoln's birth. Knowing the limitations of the Emancipation Proclamation, Lincoln urged Congress to pass a 13th Amendment outlawing slavery everywhere in the land.

A constitutional amendment requires the approval of two-thirds of Congress. Then three-fourths of the states must ratify (approve) an amendment before it can become law.

Lincoln pressured and negotiated with members of Congress until finally a vote was taken. When the required majority voted "yea," spectators cheered and wept. Lincoln called the vote a "great moral victory." It was now up to the states—and military victory—to bring a final end to slavery.

Meanwhile, the armies did their part to bring an end to the war. General Sherman left Atlanta to lead his men on an infamous "March to the Sea." His massive army commandeered food and horses. They burned buildings and destroyed remaining crops as they made their way through Georgia and South Carolina. Bloody fighting in Tennessee ended in Union victory. General Grant extended his siege lines around Petersburg, Virginia, following Lincoln's command to "hold on with a bull-dog [grip], and chew & choke, as much as possible."

Lincoln held peace talks with Confederate representatives (including his old friend from Congress, Confederate vice president Alexander Stephens), but the talks came to nothing. He held on to his faith that the great sacrifices of this terrible war were necessary. He shared his thoughts about it in a moving inaugural speech.

Though the day of his second inauguration was dark and rainy, people crowded Washington's streets and leaned from balconies to watch the inaugural procession pass. Bells rang and bands played as Lincoln made his way to a platform in front of the Capitol Building.

Just as Lincoln rose to speak, the sun burst out from behind the clouds. His words, too, seemed to offer hope for light beyond dark days. "With malice toward none," he told

VOTE FOR ME!

WHETHER YOU'RE running for student council or practicing for a future run for the presidency, here are some creative ways to campaign!

WHAT YOU NEED

- Pencil
- Paper
- Computer and printer (optional)
- Colored markers
- White poster board
- Scissors
- Pin-backs (safety pins with backing; available at sewing paper or craft stores)
- White glue
- Ruler
- Hole punch
- Elastic string
- Red, white, and blue construction paper
- Chopsticks
- Red, white, and blue balloons
- Thick, off-white

Develop a platform. In 1864, Lincoln ran on a platform that promised to pursue the war until the Confederacy surrendered, to pass a constitutional amendment abolishing slavery, and to construct a transcontinental railroad. Make a list of what you plan to do if elected.

Create a campaign slogan and logo. Dwight D. Eisenhower played on his nickname ("I Like Ike!"). William Henry Harrison and vice-presidential candidate John Tyler pointed to Harrison's exploits in the Battle of Tippecanoe with "Tippecanoe and Tyler Too!" During his second election, Lincoln's unofficial slogan was the punch line from an old joke: "Don't swap horses in the middle of the stream!" You can propose strategy ("54-40 or Fight!") or make homey promises ("A Chicken in Every Pot!"), just as long as your slogan is short and sweet. By hand or using computer software, design a logo that complements the slogan.

Make buttons, hats, pennants, posters, and postcards. Decorate by hand or use computer software to make designs for these items. For buttons, cut round circles from poster board, decorate, and glue pin-backs on the back. Cut visor-shaped hats from poster board (see drawing) and punch a hole on each side. Knot elastic string in one hole, fit the visor to your head, then knot the string in the other hole. For pennants, cut long triangles from red, white, and blue construction paper and decorate. Glue the short side of each triangle to a chopstick. Show your smiling face on a poster, along with a list of your very best qualities.

Kick off your campaign with a pretend convention. Decorate a room with red, white, and blue balloons. Hang up posters. Pass out pennants, hats, and buttons to guests. Have a friend announce your nomination for office. Make a grand speech. Play loud music.

Press the flesh (that means shake hands) and talk, talk, talk. Meet the voters. Hand out buttons and flyers. Tell everyone why they should vote for you. If you have a computer with presentation software, create a presentation outlining your goals and find opportunities to show it. Invite your opponent to a debate.

Did you win the election? Design invitations to your inaugural ball. Use off-white paper and fancy script: "The honor of your presence is requested at the ceremonies attending the inauguration of . . . *me!*"

the hushed crowd, "with charity for all; with firmness in the right, as God gives us to see the right, let us strive on to finish the work we are in; to bind up the nation's wounds; to care for him who shall have borne the battle, and for his widow, and his orphan—to do all which may achieve and cherish a just, and a lasting peace, among ourselves, and with all nations."

Among the listeners was Frederick Douglass. After the speech, Douglass came to the White House, only to be barred at the door by guards who refused to allow a black man entry. Lincoln heard and quickly sent word to let Douglass in. He shook Douglass's hand and asked him what he thought of the inaugural speech. "There is no man in the country whose opinion I value more than yours," Lin-

[LEFT] *"Lincoln's Second Inaugural"* ❖ Library of Congress [ABOVE] *John Wilkes Booth*

coln said. Douglass replied that the speech was "a sacred effort."

Another onlooker did not agree. John Wilkes Booth watched with bitter feelings as Lincoln was sworn in for a second term. The handsome, dark-haired Booth, a famous actor, lived in the North but was an ardent secessionist. He passionately hated the president. Booth and a band of fellow conspirators met often at Mary Surratt's Tavern in Maryland. They plotted to kidnap Lincoln and hold him in exchange for Southern prisoners of war. So far, their attempts had failed, but they closely watched the president's schedule and habits, hoping for another chance.

The beginning of Lincoln's second term felt as busy as his first. He selected four new members for his cabinet and a new chief justice of the Supreme Court. His office and hallways were as crowded as ever with people asking for favors, promotions, and passes to cross enemy lines. The work, worries, and sleepless nights took a toll on his health. Lincoln felt worn and weary, and always cold. One day he was so sick and tired he conducted a cabinet meeting from his bed. Mary worried about her husband. When Lincoln received an invitation from General Grant to visit the army's headquarters, she encouraged him to go. The trip would be a nice break from Washington, and they could visit their son Robert, too.

Boarding the presidential boat, the *River Queen*, the family steamed downriver to Grant's headquarters. The military camp felt like a busy city, with warehouses, hospitals, and row after row of small, white tents. The fresh air and change of scenery did Lincoln good. He visited with Robert, inspected troops, and met with officers. He took a train to examine a battlefield just hours after combat. The wretched condition of Rebel prisoners touched his heart. His kindly face deepened with sadness at the sight of Union and Confederate dead.

Back at the camp, Grant had scheduled a review of troops for the president. Lincoln rode to the grounds on horseback while Mary followed in an ambulance carriage. By the time she arrived, the review had begun. Her place of honor by her husband's side had been taken by a general's wife. Mary became enraged. Her angry words embarrassed Lincoln and made the general's wife cry. Mary spent the next few days in her cabin on the *River Queen,* then left for Washington. Once home, she felt sorry and telegraphed her husband that she would soon return. "Tad and I are both well, and will be glad to see you," Lincoln replied.

Tad, who had stayed behind with his father, loved the *River Queen*. He studied every nook and cranny of the boat while Lincoln again visited wounded soldiers at the army hospitals.

It took hours, but Lincoln shook hands with each of the men. Afterward, someone asked him whether his arm hurt from all the handshakes. In reply, Lincoln picked up an ax that was resting on a nearby woodpile and chopped for a few minutes. Then he took the heavy ax in his hand and held it out horizontally. His arm held the ax perfectly steady. When he put the ax down, several strong, young soldiers tried to do the trick but failed.

One night, Lincoln invited Generals Grant and Sherman and Admiral David Porter aboard the *River Queen*. The end of the war was coming, Lincoln told them. He wanted to

The ruins of Richmond ❧ National Archives

be sure that when the end came, the Rebels would be treated generously and welcomed back into the Union. "Let them all go, officers and all," he said. "I want no one punished; treat them liberally all round."

General Lee's Confederate army had suffered during the long siege of Petersburg. The starving men could not hold the city any longer. Their only hope was to break away from Petersburg, march to join the remaining Rebel armies, and fight elsewhere. Lee telegraphed President Jefferson Davis in the nearby Confederate capital that Richmond must be evacuated. As a Union attack surged forward, the Confederate army withdrew from Petersburg.

In Richmond, government officials hurriedly packed papers. Families rushed to get on the last trains. As people evacuated the city, they set fire to warehouses and bridges to thwart the coming Northern troops. The fires spread in a wild wind. Buildings collapsed and whole blocks and neighborhoods burned.

The next day, those Richmonders left in their burned city saw a sight they could not believe. President Abraham Lincoln, wearing his stovepipe hat, walked into Richmond holding his son Tad's hand. Loyal Confederates peered from behind curtains at the startling sight. Richmond's blacks poured into the streets. "Glory!" they shouted. "Father Abraham! We know now that we are free!" They

Lincoln visits the former home of Jefferson Davis
❖ Library of Congress

crowded around Lincoln, touching his hands and clothes. When one man knelt before him, Lincoln stopped. "Don't kneel to me," he said. "That is not right. You must kneel to God only, and thank Him for the liberty you will enjoy hereafter."

Lincoln pressed on, walking two miles to the Confederate White House. He sat in Jefferson Davis's chair and quietly asked for a drink of water. Richmond had fallen. Outside, Union troops cheered for the president.

While Grant's army pursued the exhausted Confederate troops, Lincoln returned to the *River Queen* and steamed back to Washington. He went immediately to the home of Secretary of State William Seward. Seward had been injured in a carriage accident and lay in bed with a broken jaw and arm. Lincoln stretched out beside Seward, leaned on his elbow, and told his friend everything about Richmond's fall. "I think we are near the end at last," he said. That night, Lincoln received a telegram from General Grant. Lee had surrendered his army at Appomattox Courthouse, Virginia. Other Confederate armies were still in the field, but with Lee's surrender, the end was indeed near.

"Boom, boom, boom went the guns," wrote a reporter. Windows shook as Washington celebrated the surrender with a 500-gun salute. Laughing and singing, people spilled into the streets. They crowded around the White House, calling for the president. They cheered loudly when Tad stuck his head out of a window to wave a Confederate flag. When Lincoln appeared, they threw their hats in the air and shouted for a speech. The president declined to give a speech that day, but he asked a band to play the Southern tune "Dixie." It's "one of the best tunes I have ever heard," he told the crowd.

When Lincoln gave a speech the next day, the crowd was a little disappointed. They were in the mood for celebrating and wanted

THE TOWN of Lincoln, Illinois, celebrated its 100th and 150th birthdays by burying time capsules. On the 100th anniversary of Lincoln's birth, President Theodore Roosevelt placed another time capsule in a monument at Lincoln's birthplace. It contained, among other things, a copy of the Emancipation Proclamation. You can honor a moment in time by making a time capsule!

WHAT YOU NEED

- Collection of miscellaneous items (see below)
- 3-by-5-inch index cards
- Pen
- Packing tape
- A large metal container (like a popcorn tin)
- Paints and markers (and possibly butcher paper and tape)

1. Collect small, inexpensive items that represent life today. You might include a CD, a comic strip, movie ticket stubs, a map of your town, a coin and a postage stamp from this year, an old cell phone, an action figure. Or maybe a program from a school play, or magazine pictures of the latest fashions, toys, and cars. Write each item's function on a 3-by-5 card. Tape it to the item. You might also include a grocery list or a description of what your family had for dinner last night. Add the front page from your town's paper. Don't forget a photo of yourself (with name, age, and interests on the back).

2. You might ask an adult to spray-paint the container, then you can use paints or markers to decorate it (or cover with paper and decorate). Give the capsule a name (like "Time Traveler") and write it on the lid, along with the instructions "Do not open until . . ." Choose an opening date sometime in the future.

3. Invite friends for a special sealing ceremony. Ask them to bring one small item for the capsule. Place everything inside and seal it with packing tape. Announce the opening date. Ask your guests what they think life will be like on that day.

4. Buried time capsules are often lost or destroyed so store yours in an attic or closet. Write down the capsule's storage spot and opening date in a safe place. Someday in the future someone will open your time capsule—perhaps even you!

something rousing, but instead Lincoln spoke of reconstruction and the difficulties of mending the nation. He spoke too of opening the vote to black soldiers. In the crowd was John Wilkes Booth, angry and bitter at the turn of events. "That is the last speech he will ever make!" Booth exclaimed. As Lincoln finished each page of his speech, he dropped it to the floor. Tad, at his father's feet, collected the pages as they fell.

Finally, the years of war and suffering were over. Lincoln's heart was light. One friend thought he looked as happy as a boy out of school. Over the next days, the president met with his cabinet and with General Grant to discuss plans for the future. In one meeting, Lincoln mentioned a dream in which he was in a boat, heading for an unknown shore. He thought it meant something good was about to happen. He had often had the dream on the eve of victorious battles.

Lincoln had breakfast with his son Robert, who told his father all about the surrender at Appomattox. He happily composed a note to a man who had asked for a special pass to go to Richmond, writing that "no pass is necessary now. People go & return just as they did before the war."

Late that same afternoon, Lincoln set his work aside to take a carriage ride with Mary. He was so happy that Mary said to him, "Dear husband, you almost startle me by your great cheerfulness." "And well may I feel so," Lincoln replied. "I consider this day, the war has come to a close." He went on: "We must both be more cheerful in the future, for between the war and the loss of our darling Willie, we have both been very miserable." They talked of their future, and the things they would do after his term as president ended. Perhaps, Lincoln thought, they would travel overseas. He wanted to go to California too, to see the gold miners at work. And then perhaps they would settle down again, in Chicago or back in Springfield.

That day, Washington's newspapers announced that "the President and his Lady will be at the Theatre this evening." Their friends Major Henry Rathbone and Clara Harris were to join them. Mary had a headache after their ride and wanted to cancel their plans, but Lincoln insisted they go. He did not want to disappoint the people who might go to Ford's Theatre just to see him. He was sure, too, that there would be no rest for him if he spent the evening at the White House.

When John Wilkes Booth heard of the Lincolns' plan for the evening, he made some plans of his own. His hatred of Lincoln had grown. He wanted to kill the president! He called on his fellow conspirators and they agreed to a horrible plot. That night they would bring

"I AM ABRAHAM LINCOLN."

How many Lincolns would it take to screw in a light bulb? None—Lincoln read and worked by gaslight! But if you wanted a few Lincolns to light the way, you could find plenty through the Association of Lincoln Presenters.

Across the country, more than 120 dedicated reenactors grow beards and wear black suits, stovepipe hats, and uncomfortable boots. They stand a little stoop-shouldered as they speak in the persona of Abraham Lincoln to school groups and at museums. Sometimes they are accompanied by a perfectly dressed Mary Todd. These presenters do more than study history—they walk and talk it.

You might see a Lincoln presenter at one of the hundreds of Civil War reenactments held in the United States every year. Participants live in encampments and act out Civil War battles. Visitors are welcome to tour the camps and talk to officers and soldiers (unless they are playing dead on the battlefield!). It is a great way to learn about history.

Lincoln presenters spend long hours studying and preparing for their role. They might suffer from sore feet or have trouble gluing on bushy eyebrows. One presenter scared a little girl who thought he really was Abraham Lincoln, "dead but still walking around!" But they are dedicated to keeping Abraham Lincoln's legacy—and his compassion, humor, and honesty—alive.

Lincoln presenters ❖ Vicki N. Shaw-Woodard

down the federal government by assassinating the president, the vice president, and the secretary of state. Booth armed himself with a gun and a knife.

Lincoln's advisers had warned him to be more careful. They assigned him an escort but, uncomfortable having guards, Lincoln often went out alone or with friends. Though

PAINT A PANORAMIC BACKDROP

THE PLAY Lincoln saw at Ford's Theatre, a comedy about an American bumpkin and his high-class English relatives, took place on a British estate. Its scene changes included the manor's drawing room, chamber room, library, office, and wine cellar as well as a rural cottage. Any stage crew member will tell you that such scene changes are a lot of work!

For this activity, you will adapt a style of painting that was popular in Lincoln's time to use as a moving backdrop for your own play. "Moving panoramas" were paintings on long canvases that were mounted on two spools. With the turn of a crank, the painting moved from one spool to the other. A picture story unfolded before the eyes of the viewers. Write a play, and then use this method for easy scene changes.

WHAT YOU NEED

- A script
- Butcher paper on a spool, 36 inches wide, with length depending on the number of scenes (8 feet per scene)
- Pencils
- Erasers
- Tempera paints
- Brushes
- Thick, round pole (a broom handle would work)
- White glue or masking tape
- Friends (two to move the backdrop; others to act and to watch the play)

Plan the scenes you will need for your play. For each scene, you will make an eight foot-long backdrop. Unroll nine feet of paper for the first scene and lay it flat on the floor.

Lightly sketch the scenery in pencil, leaving six inches of white space on the left and right sides of the backdrop. (Note: the paper is not wide enough to make a floor-to-ceiling backdrop. Yours will show scenes from the waist up.) When you are happy with your drawings, use paint to complete the scene. Let dry thoroughly. Glue the end of the paper to the pole and let the glue dry. Alternately, you could use masking tape. Carefully roll the backdrop onto the pole, leaving the next nine feet of white paper on the floor. Pencil in the next scene, paint, let dry, and continue until all the scenes are completed. Carefully roll the paintings back on to the butcher paper spool.

Gather your audience and let the show begin! Have one friend hold the spool of paper and another hold the pole. When the first scene ends, the friend holding the pole should roll up the scenery until Scene Two shows. (It takes strength to hold the backdrops for long, so make sure you include intermissions—short breaks—in your play.)

he had a drawerful of threatening letters, Lincoln felt no one really meant him harm. On this night, a single bodyguard was assigned to stand guard outside the president's box at the theater.

The Lincolns and their guests arrived at the theater a bit late. As they entered, the audience stood and cheered, and the orchestra struck up a rousing version of "Hail to the Chief." The foursome took their seats in a special balcony box and the play, a comedy called *Our American Cousin*, resumed. One of the actors got a laugh from the Lincolns and the audience when he made up a line referring to the president's reputation for telling jokes. "That reminds me of a little story . . ." the actor said. Mary happily moved close to her husband. "What will Miss Harris think of my hanging on to you so?" she asked him. Lincoln smiled. "She won't think anything about it," he said.

No one questioned John Wilkes Booth when he entered the theater and climbed the winding stairs to the president's box. He was well known by all the staff, having acted in plays at Ford's Theatre before. Lincoln's guard had stepped away from his post outside the door. Booth gave his calling card to an attendant standing nearby, opened the door to the box, stepped in, and pulled out a gun.

Booth knew the play and had planned his moment. One of the actors delivered a comic

Ford's Theatre ❖ Ford's Theatre National Historic Site

line; the audience laughed loudly. Booth drew up his arm and pulled the trigger. The sound of gunfire was masked by laughter. Only when Mary screamed did people realize that something had happened. They looked up to see smoke drifting from the president's box and Major Rathbone desperately wrestling a man armed with a knife. Then a woman cried out, "The president has been shot!"

Booth stabbed Rathbone, then leaped from the balcony to the stage. He landed badly, snapping a bone in his ankle, and hobbled offstage. "Sic semper tyrannis!" he cried (a Latin phrase meaning "thus ever to tyrants"), and "The South is avenged!" The stunned audi-ence sat silent for one moment, then shouted, "Booth! Get him! Hang him!" But Booth escaped into the alley, climbed onto his waiting horse, and galloped into the cold and foggy night.

At the same time, conspirator Lewis Powell fought his way into Secretary Seward's home. He attacked Seward's son and other members of his household, then brutally stabbed Seward in his bed, leaving him badly wounded but still alive. The man assigned to kill Vice President Johnson backed out of the deed at the last moment.

Word of the terrible events spread quickly. Military patrols combed the city. Back at Ford's Theatre, a crowd of shocked and griev-

[LEFT] *John Wilkes Booth fleeing after shooting Lincoln* [BELOW] *"The president is no more"* ❖ Ford's Theatre National Historic Site

134

ing people gathered in the street. Lincoln had been shot in the head; the first doctors to reach him knew immediately that the wound was deadly. They ordered him carried to a house across the street from the theater, and laid his long body diagonally on a bed.

Poor Mary cried and called to her husband through the long, awful night. Robert arrived, and soon doctors, friends, and members of Lincoln's staff and cabinet crowded the little room. Outside, it began to rain. As the night passed and dawn arrived, Lincoln's breath grew shallower. Finally, it was over. "The president is no more," a doctor stated, and all fell silent. Secretary of War Edwin Stanton, at the foot of Lincoln's bed, tears streaming down his face, was the first to speak. "Now he belongs to the ages," he said.

"The whole world bowed their heads in grief when Abraham Lincoln died," wrote Mary's friend Elizabeth Keckley. Across the nation, bells tolled and flags were lowered to half-mast. People gathered in churches and on street corners, feeling shocked and helpless. Soldiers wrapped black bands around their arms in honor of their Father Abraham. In Washington, the celebrations held only days earlier seemed like a distant dream. Now the buildings and houses were draped in black and people lingered outside the White House, weeping.

 # HONOR ABRAHAM LINCOLN

Many monuments honor the 16th president. Societies across the country are dedicated to studying Lincoln's life. Museums, newsletters, and thousands of books tell his story. In 1909, his 100th birthday was celebrated with the introduction of the Lincoln penny. A new penny, with four designs for the reverse side of the coin, will be issued in 2009 to honor Lincoln's 200th birthday. Communities across the nation will celebrate this birthday with parades, performances, and special exhibits.

Here are 16 ways you can honor the memory of this great president! Can you think of more?

- Memorize the Gettysburg Address.
- Measure your height.
- See a Lincoln presenter or a Civil War reenactment.
- Walk six miles to borrow a book.
- Start a Lincoln Club to discuss Civil War history and books about the 16th president.
- Visit Lincoln sites in person or take a virtual tour of New Salem and Springfield sites (see "Web Sites to Explore").
- Tell a joke!
- Play baseball (Lincoln loved it).
- Settle a difference between friends.
- Read the newspaper.
- Collect pennies.
- Ride a train.
- Play leapfrog.
- Read Shakespeare out loud.
- Plant a flower.
- Share your concerns with the current president (The White House, 1600 Pennsylvania Ave., Washington, DC 20502, (202) 456-1414, comments@whitehouse.gov), or with your senators and members of the House of Representatives.

After a funeral service at the White House, a mournful procession brought Lincoln's body to the Capitol Building. Marching soldiers led the way, followed by officers on horseback. Behind Lincoln's hearse were the black carriages of diplomats and officials, then a long procession of military bands and civic associations. A spontaneous crowd of sorrowful black citizens and wounded soldiers, bandaged and on crutches, brought up the rear. Tens of thou-

"Die when I may, I want it said of me by those who know me best that I always plucked a thistle and planted a flower where I thought a flower would grow."
—Abraham Lincoln

[BELOW] *President Lincoln's funeral processio* ❖ Library of Congress
[RIGHT] *Lincoln is buried, Springfield, Illinois*
❖ Library of Congress

sands inched through the Capitol Building to view and honor their president.

Lincoln's casket, along with that of his beloved son Willie, was carried across the country on a special nine-car funeral train. Robert accompanied the train but Mary stayed in Washington, too grief-stricken to leave her room. Tad, devastated, stayed behind with his mother. Eleven mournful funerals were held in cities across the nation.

As the train passed small towns and communities, people knelt beside the tracks and bowed their heads. At night, they lit bonfires along its route. At a final service in Springfield, grief-stricken friends and neighbors said their last good-byes. Then Lincoln's horse Old Bob followed the hearse to the cemetery, where Abraham Lincoln and his son Willie were laid to rest.

[LEFT] *"President Abraham Lincoln, in a photograph taken four days before his death*
❖ Library of Congress
[RIGHT] *Lincoln Memorial at Night"*
❖ Terry J. Adams, National Park Service

WHAT HAPPENED NEXT?

 Stepmother Sarah Bush Lincoln, too weak to attend Lincoln's burial in Springfield, stayed at her Illinois farm until her death in 1869.

 William Herndon, Lincoln's old law partner, gave lectures about Lincoln and later published a book about the president's life.

 Springfield friend Joshua Speed had turned down jobs in Lincoln's administration but helped with Union activities in Kentucky during the war.

 Former debate rival Stephen A. Douglas died of typhoid just a month after holding Lincoln's hat at the first inauguration.

 Mary Owens, Lincoln's former love, married and had three children. Her husband died in the Civil War. She never regretted saying no to Lincoln's proposal of marriage.

 Dedicated assistants John Hay and John Nicolay wrote a 10-volume history of Abraham Lincoln. Hay became an ambassador, then secretary of state. Nicolay became a diplomat, and a marshal of the Supreme Court.

 Andrew Johnson was sworn in as 17th president of the United States. Secretary of State Seward recovered from his wounds and served in President Johnson's cabinet, as did Secretary of War Edwin Stanton.

 Frederick Douglass worked for the rest of his life on behalf of civil rights for blacks and for women.

 Lincoln's favorite general, Ulysses S. Grant, became president, serving from 1869 to 1877. Former general George McClellan became governor of New Jersey.

 Robert E. Lee became president of Washington College (later renamed Washington and Lee University). Jefferson Davis was captured by Federal troops and imprisoned for two years. He later wrote a history of the Confederate government.

 John Wilkes Booth was caught and killed by Federal troops as he hid in a Virginia tobacco barn. Eight accomplices were arrested. Four, including Lewis Powell and Mary Surratt, were hanged.

 Robert Todd Lincoln became secretary of war, ambassador to Great Britain, then president of the Pullman Train Company.

 Mary and Tad Lincoln lived for a time in Europe, then moved to Chicago. Tad fell ill and died at only 18 years of age. Mary was briefly committed to an asylum. She spent her last years at her sister's home in Springfield.

 For many years, Abraham Lincoln did not rest in peace. Grave robbers tried to steal his casket, planning to demand a ransom for its return. They were caught in the act and imprisoned. Authorities hid, moved, opened, and reburied the coffin several times until, at Robert Lincoln's request, Lincoln was reburied beneath 10 feet of concrete.

 The country stumbled through its grief—for Lincoln and for the 620,000 who had given their lives during the four long years of war. Soldiers returned home. Their nation had, as Lincoln had predicted, experienced "a new birth of freedom." The 13th Amendment to the Constitution was ratified, outlawing slavery forever. The Union that had come so close to disintegrating had, thanks to the leadership of Abraham Lincoln, endured.

ABRAHAM LINCOLN SITES TO VISIT

Abraham Lincoln Birthplace National Historic Site

2995 Lincoln Farm Road
Hodgenville, Kentucky 42748
(270) 358-3137
www.nps.gov/abli

❖ Climb up 56 steps (one for each year of Lincoln's life) to a marble temple, home to a modest log cabin representing Lincoln's birthplace. Walk through the woods and imagine life here in 1809, the year Abraham Lincoln was born. His father named this Sinking Spring Farm; the spring (which the Lincolns used for their water) still flows at the base of the temple.

Abraham Lincoln Boyhood Home

U.S. 31E
Hodgenville, Kentucky 42748
(270) 358-3137
www.nps.gov/abli

❖ The Lincoln family lived here, on Knob Creek Farm, from 1811 to 1816. Young Abraham fished and helped his father plant corn and pumpkins. A cabin now standing on the site contains some logs from a cabin built in Lincoln's time. Walk the land and view the steep hills that gave the Lincoln farm its name.

Abraham Lincoln Presidential Library and Museum

212 North Sixth Street
Springfield, Illinois 62701
(217) 558-8844
www.alplm.org

❖ Plan to spend a whole day (or more) at this museum! Inspect a replica of Lincoln's boyhood cabin and walk through an 1860s White House, from kitchen to Cabinet Room. Have your photo taken with the Lincoln family and stop by "Mrs. Lincoln's Attic" to try on period dresses or Union or Confederate uniforms. Watch the "Civil War in Four Minutes," see modern-day campaign commercials for Lincoln and his rivals, and don't miss the spooky, high-tech presentation "Ghosts in the Library."

Chicago History Museum

1601 North Clark Street
Chicago, Illinois 60614
(312) 642-4600
www.chicagohs.org

❖ The city where Lincoln was nominated for the presidency is proud of its state's favorite son. Visit this museum to see a variety of Lincoln artifacts, including his well-loved stovepipe hat and the bed in which he died.

Ford's Theatre National Historic Site

511 10th Street NW
Washington, D.C. 20004
(202) 426-6924
www.nps.gov/foth

❖ Join a ranger-led talk to hear about the tragic events of April 14, 1865. View the president's box, visit the building's museum, and cross the street to see the boardinghouse where Abraham Lincoln died. Today, plays are held once again at Ford's Theatre.

Gettysburg National Military Park

97 Taneytown Road
Gettysburg, Pennsylvania 17325
(717) 334-1124
www.nps.gov/gett

❖ Here, at the site of the largest Civil War battle, Abraham Lincoln delivered his profound Gettysburg Address, honoring "those who . . . gave their lives that that nation might live." Plan sev-

eral days for visiting the visitor's center, the battlegrounds, and the cemetery that Lincoln dedicated.

Indiana History Center

450 West Ohio Street
Indianapolis, Indiana 46202
(317) 232-1882
www.indianahistory.org

❖ Visit more than once to see "The Faces of Lincoln," a permanent exhibition featuring rotating materials. See Lincoln up close and personal with his family or as he leads his country through its greatest crisis.

Lincoln Boyhood National Memorial

3027 East South Street
Lincoln City, Indiana 47552
(812) 937-4541
www.nps.gov/libo

❖ Watch films and view period artifacts at the museum, then hike to the site of the Lincoln family cabin (you'll pass the grave of Nancy Hanks Lincoln along the way). At the replica cabin and farm, costumed interpreters demonstrate how the pioneer family lived and worked. As they plant, hoe and harvest, care for livestock,

and keep house, you might wonder how young Lincoln found time to read!

Lincoln-Herndon Law Offices State Historic Site

Sixth and Adams Streets
Springfield, Illinois 62701
(217) 785-7289
www.illinoishistory.gov/hs/lincoln_herndon.htm

❖ It may not be quite as messy as it was in the days when Lincoln and his partner William Herndon worked here, but their one-time law office has been restored with period furnishings. Take a guided tour and learn about Lincoln's pre-presidential work life.

Lincoln Home National Historic Site

426 South Seventh Street
Springfield, Illinois 62701
(217) 492-4241 x221
www.nps.gov/liho

❖ Stop at the visitor's center to see an orientation film, then tour the two-story house where Abraham Lincoln resided for 17 years. The home has been restored to its 1860s appearance; some of the furnishings actually belonged to the Lincoln family! Walk around the neighborhood to visit other period homes and the railroad depot where Lincoln said goodbye to his Springfield neighbors.

Lincoln Memorial
23rd Street NW
Washington, D.C. 20024
(202) 426-6841
www.nps.gov/linc

❖ You can see the Lincoln Memorial every day—just look on the back of a penny! But it's really impressive to see in person. Built to look like an ancient Greek temple, the memorial's 36 columns represent the number of states at the time of Lincoln's death. Inside are murals, engravings of the Gettysburg Address and Lincoln's second inaugural address, and a 19-foot, 175-ton sculpture of Abraham Lincoln. Four million visitors a year pay tribute to Lincoln by visiting this site.

Lincoln Museum
200 East Berry Street
Fort Wayne, Indiana 46802
(260) 455-3864
www.thelincolnmuseum.org

❖ Learn about Lincoln's life, from the prairies to the White House, in the 11 galleries of this museum. See personal belongings like Lincoln's shawl or the pocketknife he used to slice apples. Visit interactive exhibits and four theaters. Try the challenging questions on the "Thinkin' Lincoln" Wall, solve history mysteries in the Curiosity Corner, or become a curator for a day.

Lincoln's New Salem State Historic Site
15588 History Lane
Petersburg, Illinois 62675
(217) 632-4000
www.lincolnsnewsalem.com

❖ An entire village has been restored to show how Abraham Lincoln and his New Salem neighbors lived. This living museum's buildings are exact reproductions of the originals. Visit the mill, the blacksmith's shop, Rutledge Tavern, the schoolhouse, and the log cabins of residents, as well as Lincoln's store. Friendly reenactors and special events celebrate Lincoln and his era. You can even camp here!

Lincoln Tomb State Historic Site
Oak Ridge Cemetery
Springfield, Illinois 62702
(217) 782-2717
www.illinoishistory.gov/hs/lincoln_tomb.htm

❖ Abraham Lincoln is buried here with Mary Todd and three of their four children. At the entrance of this stirring memorial is a bronze bust of Lincoln; inside, statues commemorate different eras of Lincoln's life.

Mary Todd Lincoln House
578 West Main Street
Lexington, Kentucky 40507
(859) 233-9999
www.cr.nps.gov/nr/travel/lexington/mtl.htm

❖ Find out how a well-to-do family of the 1830s lived. When you tour this splendid home, you will see original furnishings and artifacts belonging to the Todd and Lincoln families. On your way upstairs, stop on the landing where Lincoln liked to stretch out and read!

Old State Capitol State Historic Site
Fifth and Adams Streets
Springfield, Illinois 62701
(217) 782-4836
www.illinoishistory.gov/hs/old_capitol.htm

❖ Put yourself back in time at Illinois's old statehouse and imagine lawyer Lincoln pleading legal cases in its chambers. Imagine the resounding cheers as he gave his "house divided" speech here in 1858. It was here, too, that Lincoln's coffin was placed so his neighbors could offer their final farewells.

President Lincoln and Soldiers' Home National Monument
Opening February 2008. Until then, contact:
3700 North Capitol Street NW
Washington, D.C. 20317
(202) 829-0436
www.lincolncottage.org

❖ Lincoln lived here during the summers of his presidency. At the time, the Soldiers' Home was a distant retreat from the commotion of the city, and a refuge from summer's heat. Starting in the fall of 2007, you can visit the restored Lincoln Cottage, where Lincoln read Shakespeare to friends.

WEB SITES TO EXPLORE

Abraham Lincoln Bicentennial 2009

www.lincolnbicentennial.gov

❖ Looking for ways to celebrate Lincoln's 200th birthday? Visit this site for the latest news on events being planned around the country.

Abraham Lincoln Online

www.showcase.netins.net/web/creative/lincoln.html

❖ Get your Lincoln questions answered here. Find the latest news about all things Lincoln; check out the Lincoln awards and scholarships for students; and enjoy a little time-travel by clicking on "Today in Lincoln's Life."

Abraham Lincoln Presidential Library and Museum

www.alincoln-library.com

❖ Click on "Museum" to get a virtual peek at this amazing, state-of-the-art museum (but try to visit in person, too).

African-American Odyssey

memory.loc.gov/ammem/aaohtml/aohome.html

❖ Maps, photographs, and artifacts tell the story of the African American people as they struggled to make their place in American society. Follow their story, from the days of Nat Turner to those of Martin Luther King Jr.

The American Civil War Homepage

sunsite.utk.edu/civil-war/warweb.html

❖ Stop here for anything you might want to know about the Civil War—including battle histories, biographies, maps, and a whole lot about Abraham Lincoln.

American Rhetoric

www.americanrhetoric.com

❖ Text, audio, and video of more than 5,000 speeches can be viewed at this site. Watch Martin Luther King Jr. give his inspiring "I have a dream" speech, view footage of John F. Kennedy giving his inaugural speech, and listen to recordings of Lincoln's Gettysburg Address (re-created by famous actors).

America's Library

www.americaslibrary.gov

❖ Get comfy, because you'll want to spend hours here. You can "Meet Amazing Americans," "Explore the States," and "Jump Back in Time" to any era in American history. Take part in a presidential scavenger hunt, help dynamite Mount Rushmore, or become a history super sleuth!

The Democracy Project

pbskids.org/democracy

❖ This special site for kids shows how government affects you. You can learn the secret history of presidents, "Step Inside the Voting Booth," and find out what it's like to "Be President for a Day."

Lincoln's New Salem

www.lincolnsnewsalem.com

Lincoln Home National Historic Site

www.nps.gov/liho/home/home.htm

❖ Get a peek at Lincoln's pre-presidential life by taking virtual tours of the village of New Salem and the Lincoln family's Springfield home.

The Underground Railroad

www.nationalgeographic.com/railroad

❖ "You are a slave," this site begins. Do you have the courage to make your way to freedom? Find out what it was like to follow Harriet Tubman, seek out safe houses in an unknown land, and cross icy lakes to Canada.

Understanding Slavery

school.discovery.com/schooladventures/slavery/world.html

❖ Learn about the history of slavery throughout the world. Follow Olaudah Equiano, a captured African of the Ibo people who found his way to freedom. Witness an 1845 slave auction and click on each person present to find out how his or her actions could oppose or contribute to the institution of slavery.

The White House

www.whitehouse.gov

❖ Read bios of presidents, learn about White House traditions, and have fun with games and quizzes on the special "Kids" pages. "History and Tours" will lead you through life in the White House, past and present.

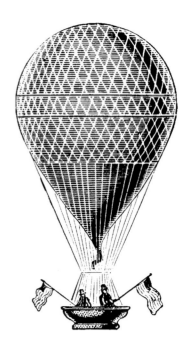

BIBLIOGRAPHY

Burlingame, Michael, ed. *Lincoln Observed: Civil War Dispatches of Noah Brooks*. Baltimore: Johns Hopkins University Press, 1998.

Catton, Bruce. *The Civil War*. New York: Houghton Mifflin, 1988.

Davis, James E. *Frontier Illinois*. Bloomington, IN: Indiana University Press, 1998.

Donald, David Herbert. *Lincoln*. New York: Simon & Schuster, 1995.

Donald, David Herbert. *Lincoln at Home*. New York: Simon & Schuster, 1999.

Donald, David Herbert. *"We Are Lincoln Men": Abraham Lincoln and His Friends*. New York: Simon & Schuster, 2003.

Fehrenbacher, Don E., ed. *Lincoln: Speeches and Writings 1832–1858*. New York: Library of America, 1989.

Fehrenbacher, Don E., ed. *Lincoln: Speeches and Writings 1859–1865*. New York: Library of America, 1989.

Gates, Henry Louis Jr., ed. *Frederick Douglass: Autobiographies*. New York: Library of America, 1994.

Gienapp, William E. *Abraham Lincoln and Civil War America*. New York: Oxford University Press, 2002.

Goodwin, Doris Kearns. *Team of Rivals: The Political Genius of Abraham Lincoln*. New York: Simon & Schuster, 2005.

Herndon, William Henry. *Herndon's Life of Lincoln*. New York: Da Capo Press, 1983.

Holzer, Harold, ed. *Lincoln As I Knew Him: Gossip, Tributes and Revelations from His Best Friends and Worst Enemies*. Chapel Hill, NC: Algonquin Books of Chapel Hill, 1999.

Johannsen, Robert W. *Stephen A. Douglas*. New York: Oxford University Press, 1973.

Keckley, Elizabeth. *Behind the Scenes: Or, Thirty Years a Slave, and Four Years in the*

White House. New York: Oxford University Press, 1988.

Klein, Maury. *Days of Defiance*. New York: Alfred A. Knopf, 1997.

Kunhardt, Philip B. Jr., Philip B. Kunhardt III, and Philip W. Kunhardt. *Lincoln: An Illustrated Biography*. New York: Alfred A. Knopf, 1992.

McPherson, James M. *Abraham Lincoln and the Second American Revolution*. New York: Oxford University Press, 1990.

McPherson, James M. *Battle Cry of Freedom*. New York: Ballantine Books, 1988.

Oates, Stephen B. *With Malice Toward None: A Life of Abraham Lincoln*. New York: HarperCollins, 1994.

Perret, Geoffrey. *Lincoln's War: The Untold Story of America's Greatest President as Commander in Chief*. New York: Random House, 2004.

Pinkser, Matthew. *Lincoln's Sanctuary: Abraham Lincoln and the Soldiers' Home*. New York: Oxford University Press, 2003.

Staudenraus, P. J., ed. *Mr. Lincoln's Washington: Selections from the Writings of Noah Brooks,*

Civil War Correspondent. South Brunswick, NJ: Thomas Yoseloff, 1967.

Wagner, Margaret E., Gary W. Gallagher, and Paul Finkelman, eds. *The Library of Congress Civil War Desk Reference*. New York: Simon & Schuster, 2002.

Waugh, John C. *Reelecting Lincoln: The Battle for the 1864 Presidency*. New York: Crown Publishers, 1997.

Whitman, Walt. "Abraham Lincoln." In *The Norton Reader*, edited by Arthur M. Eastman. New York: W. W. Norton, 1992. 79–82.

Whitman, Walt. "Death of Abraham Lincoln." In *The Norton Reader*, edited by Arthur M. Eastman. New York: W. W. Norton, 1992. 186–197.

Wiles, David. "Lincoln Breaks the Ice." *Civil War Times*, February 2002, 30–57.

Wilson, Douglas L. *Honor's Voice: The Transformation of Abraham Lincoln*. New York: Alfred A. Knopf, 1998.

Winik, Jay. *April 1865: The Month That Saved America*. New York: HarperCollins, 2001.

Zall, P. M. *Abe Lincoln Laughing*. Berkeley: University of California Press, 1982.

INDEX

MORE BOOKS FROM JANIS HERBERT

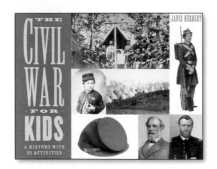

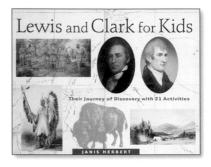

Civil War for Kids
A History with 21 Activities

By Janis Herbert

"For children who really want to know what it felt like to take an active role in the past, The Civil War for Kids *is it!"*
—Civil War Book Review

"This book provides a look at the Civil War and its leaders and includes activities such as battle reenactments and recipes for soldiers' rations. . . . Ideal for classrooms."
—School Library Journal

Ages 9 & up
Two-color interior
$14.95 (CAN $22.95)
ISBN-13: 978-1-55652-355-7
ISBN-10: 1-55652-355-6

Leonardo da Vinci for Kids
His Life and Ideas, 21 Activities

By Janis Herbert

✳ Selected by the Children's Book Council and the National Council for Social Studies as a Notable Social Studies Trade Book for Young People

"The high-quality reproductions of the artist's sketches and paintings coupled with an interesting text give readers a full picture of this truly amazing man."
—School Library Journal

Kids will understand the important discoveries that da Vinci made through inspiring activities that celebrate the marriage of art and science.

Ages 8 & up
Four-color interior
$16.95 (CAN $25.95)
ISBN-13: 978-1-55652-298-7
ISBN-10: 1-55652-298-3

The American Revolution for Kids
A History with 21 Activities

By Janis Herbert

✳ A Smithsonian Notable Book for Children

"The dramatic events that lay behind the Founding Fathers' struggle for liberty are vividly recounted in Herbert's lively survey."
—Smithsonian

The true accounts of those who created the United States come to life in this activity book celebrating freedom and democracy.

Ages 9 & up
Two-color interior
$14.95 (CAN $22.95)
ISBN-13: 978-1-55652-456-1
ISBN-10: 1-55652-456-0

Lewis and Clark for Kids
Their Journey of Discovery with 21 Activities

By Janis Herbert

"This book invites readers to join Lewis and Clark's epic journey and helps them make their own discoveries along the way."
—Dayton Duncan, cowriter and coproducer of the PBS documentary *Lewis and Clark: The Journey of the Corps of Discovery*

These 21 activities bring to life the Lewis and Clark expedition, an exploratory mission across a continent full of unique plants and animals, native cultures, and great adventure.

Ages 9 & up
Two-color interior
$14.95 (CAN $22.95)
ISBN-13:978-1-55652-374-8
ISBN-10: 1-55652-374-2

Available at your favorite bookstore or by calling (800) 888-4741.

CHICAGO REVIEW PRESS

Distributed by
Independent Publishers Group
www.ipgbook.com

www.chicagoreviewpress.com